KB040283

5 Step English

The Old Man and the Sea
Level 4-5

낮은 단계부터 원문까지 한 권에 담은
단계 영어 | 노인과 바다 LEVEL 4-5

초　　판 | 1쇄 발행 2022년 2월 20일
개정판 | 1쇄 발행 2024년 2월 19일

원 작 자 | 어니스트 헤밍웨이
영어번역 | Steve Oh, HannahAllyse Kim
정보맵핑 | 이야기 연구소
그　　림 | 김영미
감　　수 | Jinny Lee / HannahAllyse Kim / Edmund Nai /
제 작 처 | 다온피앤피
특허출원 | 10-2020-0012558
국제출원 | PCT/KR2020/002551

펴 낸 곳 | (주)도서출판동행
펴 낸 이 | 오승근
출판등록 | 2020년 3월 20일 제2020-000005호
주　　소 | 부산광역시 부산진구 동천로109, 9층
이 메 일 | withyou@withyoubooks.com
홈페이지 | https://withyoubooks.com
카카오톡 | @동행출판사

단계별 요약정보 기술은 국내특허출원 및 PCT 국제출원을 했습니다.

ISBN 979-11-91648-14-0

낮은 단계 부터 원문까지 한 권에 담은

단계 영어

노인과 바다

Level 4-5

등항
With YouBooks

인터넷에서 사용되는 언어의 55.7%가 영어입니다. 인터넷 정보의 절반 이상이 영어로 되어있습니다. 영어 못하면 서러운 것은 인터넷에서도 마찬가지입니다. 그럼 한국어는 인터넷에서 어느 정도 차지할까요? 놀라지 마세요. 한국어는 1%도 안 되는 0.4%입니다. 영어로 정보를 해석할 수 있다는 것이 곧 55.7%의 정보를 다 접한다는 걸 의미하진 않습니다. 하지만 내가 할 수 있는데 안 하는 것과 처음부터 할 수 없는 것에는 분명 차이가 있습니다.

영어에서 "말하기, 듣기, 읽기, 쓰기" 중 어느 하나 중요하지 않은 건 없습니다. 그러나 인터넷이 일상인 우리에게 더 필요한 것은 읽기라 생각합니다. 영어 읽기는 책을 읽듯이 영어로 그냥 읽는 것이 중요합니다. 하지만 그게 말처럼 쉽지 않습니다. 해보신 분들은 아시겠지만 어려운 단어들과 긴 문장들 때문에 책장이 넘어가질 않습니다. 사전 찾지 않고 모르는 단어를 유추해보려 해도 모르는 단어가 문장마다 나오는데 어떻게 유추할 수 있겠습니까?

어려운 영어 원문을 사전 없이도, 내용을 이해하며 읽을 수 있는 책이 단계별 영어 원서입니다. 한 번 아이들이 말을 배우는 과정을 생각해 보세요. '엄마', '아빠'와 같이 몇 안 되는 단어만 말하던 아이가 시간이 지나면 말이 길어지고 내용이 깊어집니다. 그러니까 처음엔 "엄마 밥 줘" 였는데, 시간이 지나면 "엄마 내가 좋아하는 김밥 먹고 싶어요" 처럼 표현에 깊이가 생긴다는 것이죠.

하지만 여기서 중요한 사실은, 표현은 달라졌지만 말하고자 하는 핵심 내용은 같다는 것입니다. 둘 다 "음식을 먹고 싶다(또는 배고프다)"라는 게 핵심입니다.

단계별 영어 원서의 구성은 마치 아이들이 3~4년에 걸쳐서 언어가 성장하는 과정을 레벨1~5에 넣은 것과 같습니다. 레벨1이 4살 아이의 표현이라면, 레벨2는 5살 아이의 표현이라 볼 수 있습니다. 전달하고자 하는 핵심 내용은 원문과 같지만, 그것을 표현하는 방식이 레벨에 따라 달라진다는 것입니다.

레벨1은 가장 쉬운 어휘를 사용해서 문장을 짧게 만들었습니다. 레벨1을 읽고 이해할 수 있다면, 레벨2는 사전 없이도 충분히 내용을 유추하며 읽을 수 있습니다. 이게 가능하냐고요? 가능합니다. 인터넷에 넘치는 독자 후기가 이를 증명해 주고 있습니다.

다시 한번 말씀드리지만, 책은 '읽어야' 합니다. 편안한 마음으로 읽어 보세요. 해석이 틀려도 괜찮고, 오해가 생겨도 괜찮습니다. 정확한 해석을 찾는 일에 집중하지 마시고 그냥 읽어 보세요. 성인도 모국어를 틀리게 사용할 때가 있지 않습니까? 그러니 틀리는 것을 겁내지 마시고 그냥 한 번 읽어 보세요.

사실 아이들은 모국어를 틀리면서 배워갑니다. 발음도 틀리고, 어순도 틀리고, 잘못된 단어도 사용하지요. 하지만 끊임없이 사용하기에 틀린 것을 고쳐가면서 결국엔 올바른 언어로 사용하게 됩니다. 이렇듯 언어는 지속성이 중요합니다. 단계별 영어 원서는 특별한 준비작업 없이도 가볍게 책장을 열어 읽을 수 있기에 언어의 지속성을 가능하게 해주는 최적에 읽기 도구입니다. 지금 바로 레벨1을 읽어 보세요. "세상 모든 영어가 레벨1이면 좋겠어요."라고 하셨던 한 독자분의 고백을 여러분도 하시게 될 겁니다.

자, 그럼 이제 시작해 보세요

Steve Oh

"고졸 학력 30대 직장인입니다. 학생 때도 영어와는 담쌓고 살았습니다. 영어를 무기로 좋은 기회 잡는 사람들을 볼 때마다 한번은 영어를 정복하겠다고 막연히 생각했습니다. "영어 일기, 원서 읽기, 쉐도우 리딩, 토익 문제 풀이" 등 시중에 많은 영어 학습법이 있었지만, 기초가 없다 보니 힘들더군요. 사전 찾느라 한 시간에 한 페이지 겨우 할까 말까 하다 보니 금방 그만두게 됐습니다. 뜻을 유추하는 것도 앞뒤는 알고 하나만 모를 때 통하지 아예 모르면 안 되더라고요. 그러다 와디즈 통해서 단계별 영어원서 시리즈를 알게 되어 지금은 레벨1을 지나 레벨2 초입을 읽고 있습니다. 레벨1은 일단 쉬웠습니다. 모르거나 모호하게 아는 단어가 없진 않았지만, 레벨1에서는 유추할 수 있었습니다. 진도가 잘 나가다 보니 재미 붙여서 꾸준히 읽혔습니다. 레벨2로 넘어와도 아는 내용, 아는 문장이라 그런지 술술 넘어갑니다. 이런 식으로 책 한 권 읽고 추가로 나올 "단계 영어" 두세 권 더 읽고 나면 독해는 충분하겠다는 자신감이 생깁니다."

– 포천 **홍님**

"초보자가 쉽게 접근할 수 있는 책 구성이 좋았습니다. 중간마다 들어 있는 삽화도 마음에 들었어요. 쉬는 시간마다 잠깐씩 읽고 있는데 제가 아직 꾸준히 읽고 있다는 게 놀랍네요. 매번 영어 원서를 사놓고 전시만 하던 제가 이런 끈기가 있다는 것을 알게 해주셔서 고맙습니다.

저는 첫 단계를 읽을 때 모르는 단어를 사전 찾지 않고 먼저 노트에 정리만 했어요. 그리고 첫 단계를 다 읽은 뒤에 노트에 적은 단어를 찾아가며 다시 읽었습니다. 이렇게 읽으니 그다음 단계를 읽고 싶은 도전이 생겨서 좋았습니다."

– 상도동 **필릭스님**

"처음으로 산 단계 영어 시리즈입니다. <노인과 바다>처럼 권위 있는 문학상을 받은 작품이라고 하면 대체로 일반인들이 읽기가 어렵습니다. 그런데 한글로도 읽기 어려운 작품을 영어로 읽는다니 다른 세상 이야기라 생각했습니다. 하지만 단계 영어 구성이 제 마음을 붙잡았습니다. 쉬운 영어로 전체 내용을 알려주고 점차 어려운 표현으로 레벨을 올리며 반복해 결국 원문을 어렵지 않게 읽을 수 있게 해준다는 개념에 책을 구매하게 됐습니다.

우선 책 곳곳에 있는 삽화들이 좋았습니다. 특히 물고기 종류나 낚시 도구 같은 모르는 단어를 그림을 통해 알 수 있게 해줘서 글을 이해하는 데 도움이 되었고, 그림이 글 중간마다 있는 것 자체가 지루함을 줄여 주었습니다. 레벨1부터 욕심내지 않고 하루에 한 챕터씩 보고 있습니다. 모르는 단어도 있지만, 그냥 한글 소설 보듯이 추측하며 넘어가고 있습니다. 레벨의 효과가 궁금해 챕터 1에 대한 레벨별 비교를 해 봤습니다. 레벨1에서 3까지는 괜찮았는데 레벨4부터는 모르는 단어가 급격히 늘어나더군요. 하지만 내용을 이미 알고 있어 읽는 데 큰 어려움이 없었습니다. 단계별 읽기의 힘이라고 생각합니다.

단계 영어 <노인과 바다> 편은 사전 없이 높은 수준의 책을 원서로 읽을 수 있는 즐거움과 성취감을 주는 좋은 책이라 생각합니다. 특히나 문학작품은 번역으로는 전달하기 힘든 그 언어의 고유한 감성이 있다고들 합니다. 그런 점에서 단계 영어의 시도는 원작자의 의도를 더 가깝게 이해할 소중한 기회의 시작이 될 수 있다고 생각합니다. 앞으로 좋은 작품으로 다시 만날 수 있기를 기대합니다."

- 수내동 **와디즈잇님**

"아이들 졸업 선물로 준비했는데, 아이들 모두 무척 좋아했어요! 소장용 하나, 학습용 하나 두고 천천히 보고 있어요! 레벨별로 쓰인 어휘가 다르다 보니, 어휘량도 늘고 리딩 훈련에 도움이 됩니다!"

- **익명의서포터님**

한 번 상상해 보세요.

세계문학을 원서로 읽는다면, 얼마나 유익할까요?

독서가 중요한 것은 누구나 아는 사실입니다. 그 중요한 독서를 영어로 할 수 있다면 얼마나 유익할까요? 한 번 상상해보세요. 세계문학을 원서로 읽고 있는 자기 모습을 말입니다. 한 마디로 '독서'와 '영어 공부'라는 두 마리 토끼를 다 잡은 것이죠. 그런데 문제는 이게 말처럼 쉽지 않다는 것입니다.

대부분 영어 원서를 읽을 때는 책처럼 쭉 읽지 못합니다. 모르는 단어가 계속해서 나오기에 사전을 찾고 한 문장 읽고 하다 보면 이게 책을 읽는 게 아니라 그냥 영어 학습지를 푸는 모습과 같아집니다. 그렇다고 공부한 흔적만큼 책 내용이 기억에 남는 것도 아닙니다. 분명 책은 읽었지만 읽는 과정을 한 문장씩 낱개 문장으로 해석하며 읽기 때문에 2~3장 읽다 보면 어떤 내용을 읽었는지 쉽게 잊어버립니다.

『단계 영어 노인과 바다』는 독서와 영어 공부라는 두 마리 토끼를 잡게 해드립니다. 방법도 어렵지 않습니다. 다음에 나오는 4가지 방법을 따라 그냥 책 읽듯이 책장을 넘기시면 됩니다.

1 영어 공부가 아닌 책을 읽는다고 생각하세요.

이게 가장 중요한 부분입니다. 우리가 책을 읽을 때 모습을 생각해보세요. 대부분 사람이 책을 읽을 때 사전을 찾지 않고 그냥 읽습니다. 읽다 보면 모르는 단어가 이런 뜻인가 보네 하며 자연스럽게 넘어갑니다. 이렇게 단계 영어를 읽으시면 됩니다.

2 레벨1부터 읽으세요.

레벨1이 쉽게 보여도 일단 레벨1부터 읽어야 다음 단계로 수월하게 올라갈 수 있습니다. 마치 계단을 오를 때, 첫 번째 계단에 발을 내딛고 그다음 계단으로 올라가는 것처럼 말입니다. 레벨1은 쉽지만, 책을 이해하는데 뼈대가 됩니다.

3 모르는 단어가 나와도 사전을 먼저 찾지 마세요.

사전은 책을 다 읽었는데도 그 단어 때문에 책 내용이 이해가 안 되거나, 그 단어의 뜻을 정확히 알고 싶어질 때 찾으시면 됩니다.

4 레벨5까지 읽으셨다면 이제 레벨 4, 3, 2, 1 순으로 읽어보세요.

복잡한 문장들이 어떻게 간략하게 요약되는지, 내 영어 실력이 어느 정도 성장했는지를 파악할 수 있습니다.

『단계 영어 노인과 바다』는
쉬운 핵심문장부터 단계적으로 읽어
영어를 쉽게 이해할 수 있습니다.

책의 특징

01 계단으로 높은 곳을 한 걸음씩 올라가듯, 어려운 영어 원문을 레벨에 따라 한 단계씩 읽도록 만든 책입니다. 레벨에 따라 단계적으로 읽으면, 노인과 바다 영어 원문도 이해하며 읽을 수 있습니다.

02 노인과 바다 레벨 1부터 4까지 본문은 레벨 5인 원문을 자연스럽게 읽을 수 있도록 단계별 정보설계 기술로 제작되었습니다.

03 원문에서 중요한 부분만 뽑아 편집한 것이 아닌, 원문을 논리적 단계로 요약해서 만들었기에 레벨별 문단 수와 챕터 수가 원문과 거의 동일합니다.

셀프 테스트

레벨 1을 몇 장 읽어보시고, '이 정도면 읽을 수 있겠다.'라는 생각이 든다면 이 책을 시작하셔도 괜찮습니다. 만약 이 책 레벨1이 어렵다면, 조금 더 쉬운 "백설공주", "잠자는 공주"를 추천해 드립니다.

단계별 특징

LEVEL 1 가벼운 시작

구 성   원작의 본질을 쉬운 어휘와 문장으로 재구성했습니다.

효 과   영어 자신감 향상!
원문 정보를 표현할 수 있는 쉬운(필수) 단어와 문장이 당신의
영어 자신감을 한 층 성장시킬 것입니다.

빠른 도서 내용 파악
원문 핵심이 들어 있어 전체 내용을 빠르게 이해할 수 있습
니다.

성취감 형성
레벨 1은 짧고 쉽지만, 독립된 한 권의 책입니다.
레벨 1을 다 읽었다면 노인과 바다 영어 원서를 일독한 것입
니다.

LEVEL 2 핵심의 확장

구 성   원문의 주요 요소들에 서술을 추가했습니다.

효 과   독서 속도 향상!
이미 읽은 핵심 문장 구조가 있기에 레벨 1보다 빠른 속도로
읽기가 가능합니다.

LEVEL 3 서술의 추가

구 성 원작에 풍부한 서술을 더 해, 본문의 세계에 더 깊이 빠지게 합니다.

효 과 자연스러운 단어 유추
레벨 1, 2를 통해 기본 단어와 문장 구조가 파악되어 한 단계 높아진 단어와 추가된 문장들도 유추하며 읽을 수 있습니다.

LEVEL 4 원문 맛보기

구 성 복잡한 문장과 어휘를 간소화해, 원문의 의미를 명확히 이해합니다.

**자 기
신 뢰** 이미 노인과 바다를 세 번 읽은 당신에게 레벨 4는 어렵지 않게 읽을 수 있는 단계가 되었습니다.

효 과 독해 능력 향상
레벨 5 원문을 자연스럽게 읽을 수 있게 도와줍니다.

LEVEL 5 원문의 정수

드디어 원문입니다. 난생처음 보는 단어들과 관용어들을 만나게 됩니다. 하지만 두려울 필요가 없습니다. 당신에게는 레벨 4가 있습니다. 막히는 단어는 사전을 찾기 전 레벨4를 통해 유추해 보세요. 이렇게 상상하며 단어 뜻을 찾았을 때 그 단어는 오랫동안 당신의 기억 속에 자리 잡게 됩니다.

sardine

skiff

gaff

harpoon

flying fish

hook

albacore

marlin

dolphin(만새기)

oar(노)

man-of-war bird

Portuguese
man-of-war

porpoise

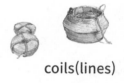

coils(lines)

sack

loggerheads

hawk-bill

green turtle

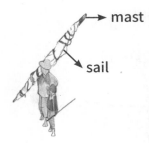
mast

sail

royal palm

mako shark

warbler

shovel-nosed shark

dark tern

cast net

<fishing hook>

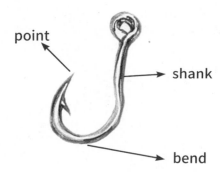

point

shank

bend

<skiff>

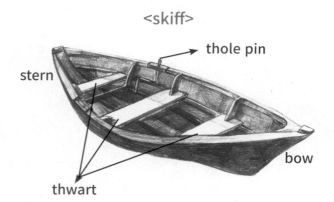

thole pin

stern

bow

thwart

Contentrds 차 례

The Old Man and the Sea LEVEL 4

The Old Man and the Sea **LEVEL 5**

Level 4는 원문의 문장을 이해할 수 있도록
단어와 구문을 쉽게 만들었어요.
Level 4를 읽고 원문인 Level 5를 읽으면
원문의 어려운 단어도 쉽게 유추할 수 있습니다.

THE ORIGINAL TEXT

"Be patient, hand," he said. "I do this for you." I wish I could feed the fish, he thought. He is my brother. But I must kill him and keep strong to do it. Slowly and conscientiously he ate all of the wedge-shaped strips of fish. He straightened up, wiping his hand on his trousers.

LEVEL 4

"Be patient, hand," he said. "I am doing this for you." "I wish I could feed the fish," he thought. "He is my brother. But I must kill him."
He ate all of the wedge-shaped strips of fish slowly and carefully. He straightened up and wiped his hand on his trousers.

The Old Man and the Sea

Chapter 1
The Old Man and the Boy

He was an old man who fished alone in a boat in the Gulf Stream. He had gone eighty-four days now without catching a fish. In the first forty days, a boy had been with him. But after forty days without a fish, the boy's parents had told him that the old man was now '**salao**', which means extremely unlucky. So the boy had to follow his parents' orders, and he took another boat.

It made the boy sad to see the old man come in each day with his boat empty. The boy always went down to help him carry either the lines or the fishing hooks and the harpoon and the sail. The sail was patched with flour sacks. It was folded and rolled. It looked like the flag of defeat.

The old man was thin and gaunt with deep wrinkles in the back of his neck. The brown spots of skin cancer, which was not harmful, from the sun's reflection on the tropical sea were on his cheeks. The spots had spread to the sides of his face, and his hands had deep scars from handling

heavy fish on the cords. But none of these scars were fresh. They were as old as markings in the desert sand.

Everything about him was old except his eyes. His eyes were the same color as the sea and they were bright and powerful.

"Santiago," the boy said to him as they climbed the bank from where the boat was parked. "I could go with you again. We've made some money."

The old man had taught the boy how to fish, and the boy loved him.

"No," the old man said. "You're with a lucky boat. Stay with them."

"But remember how you went eighty-seven days without fish, and then we caught big ones every day for three weeks."

"I remember," the old man said. "I know you did not

leave me because you doubted."

"It was Papa who made me leave. I am a boy, and I must obey him."

"I know," the old man said. "It is quite normal."

"He hasn't much faith."

"No," the old man said. "But we have. Haven't we?"

"Yes," the boy said. "Can I offer you a beer on the Terrace, and then we'll take the stuff home."

"Why not?" the old man said. "Between fishermen."

They sat on the Terrace, and many of the fishermen made fun of the old man, and he was not angry. Others looked at him and were sad. But they did not show it, and they spoke gently about the steady good weather and of what they had seen.

Chapter 2
Friendship

The successful fishermen of that day were already back. They had killed their marlin and cleaned them out. They laid the marlin across two boards and carried them to the fish house where they waited for the ice truck to carry them to the market in Havana.

Those who had caught sharks had taken them to the shark factory on the other side of the small bay where they were lifted on a block and tackle. The fishermen removed their livers, cut off their fins, skinned them, and sliced them up.

When the wind was in the east, a smell came across the harbor from the shark factory. But today there was only a slight smell because the wind had blown into the north and then died down. It was pleasant and sunny on the Terrace.

"Santiago," the boy said.

"Yes," the old man said. He was holding his glass and thinking of many years ago.

"Can I go out to get sardines for you for tomorrow?"

"No. Go and play baseball. Rogelio will throw the net for me."

"I would like to go. If I cannot fish with you. I would like to serve in some way."

"You bought me a beer," the old man said. "You are already a man."

"How old was I when you first took me in a boat?"
"Five, and you nearly died when I brought in a big fish and he nearly tore the boat to pieces. Can you remember?"
"I can remember the tail slapping and banging and the seat breaking and the clubbing noise. I can remember you throwing me into the front of the boat and feeling the whole boat shiver and the noise of you clubbing him and the sweet blood smell all over me."

"Can you really remember that or did I just tell it to you?"
"I remember everything from when we first went together."
The old man looked at him with trusting and loving eyes.
"If you were my boy I'd take you out and have an adventure," he said. "But you are your father's and your mother's and you are in a lucky boat."

"May I get the sardines? I know where I can get four baits too."
"I have mine left from today. I put them in salt in the box."
"Let me get four fresh ones."
"One is okay," the old man said. His hope and confidence had never gone, but they were becoming fresher.
"Two," the boy said.
"Two," the old man agreed. "You didn't steal them?"
"I would," the boy said. "But I bought these."
"Thank you," the old man said. Because he was

a simple person, he never thought about when he achieved humility. But he knew he had achieved it and he was not embarrassed. He still had his true pride.

"Tomorrow is going to be a good day with this current," he said.

"Where are you going?" the boy asked.

"Far out, to come in when the wind shifts. I want to be out before it is light."

"I'll try to get him to work far out," the boy said. "Then if you hook something truly big we can come to your aid."

"He does not like to work too far out."

"No," the boy said. "But I will see something that he cannot see such as a bird working and get him to come out after dolphin."

"Are his eyes that bad?"

"He is almost blind."

"It is strange," the old man said. "He never went turtle-ing. That is what kills the eyes."

"But you went turtle-ing for years near the Mosquito Coast. And your eyes are good."

"I am a strange old man."

"But are you strong enough now for a truly big fish?"

"I think so. And there are many tricks."

"Let us take the stuff home," the boy said. "So I can get the cast net and go after the sardines."

They picked up the gear from the boat. The old man carried the mast on his shoulder and the boy carried the wooden box with the coiled, hard brown lines, the gaff, and the harpoon with its bar. The box with the baits was under the back of the boat with the club that was used to overcome the big fish. No one would steal from the old man but it was better to take the sail and the heavy lines home. The old man thought leaving a gaff and a harpoon in a boat were needless temptations.

Chapter 3
The Shack

They walked up the road together to the old man's hut and went in through its open door. The old man leaned the mast with its rolled sail against the wall. The boy put the box and the other gear beside it. The mast was nearly as long as the one room of the hut.

The hut was made of the tough budshields of the royal palm which are called **guano** and in it there was a bed, a table, one chair, and a place to cook on the dirt floor. On the brown walls of the overlapping leaves of the strong **guano**, there was a picture in color of the Sacred Heart of Jesus and another of the Virgin of Cobre. These belonged to his wife. Once there was a colored photograph of his wife on the wall, but he took it off because it made him too lonely to see it. The picture was on the shelf in the corner under his clean shirt.

"What do you have to eat?" the boy asked.

"A pot of yellow rice with fish. Do you want some?"

"No, I will eat at home. Do you want me to make the fire?"

"No. I will make it later on, or I may eat the rice cold."

"May I take the cast net?"

"Of course."

There was no cast net and the boy remembered when they had sold it. But they went through this fiction every day. There was no pot of yellow rice and fish.

"Eighty-five is a lucky number," the old man said. "How would you like to see me bring in a fish that cleaned out over a thousand pounds?"

"I'll get the cast net and go get sardines. Will you sit in the sun in the doorway?"

"Yes. I have yesterday's paper and I will read the baseball section."

The boy did not know if yesterday's paper was fiction too. But the old man brought it out from under the bed.

"Perico gave it to me at the bodega," he explained.

"I'll be back when I have the sardines. I'll keep yours and mine together on ice and we can share them in the morning. When I come back you can tell me about the baseball game."

"The New York Yankees cannot lose."

"But I fear the Cleveland Indians."

"Have faith in the Yankees my son. Think of the great DiMaggio."

"I fear both the Detroit Tigers and the Cleveland Indians."

"Be careful or you will fear even the Cincinnati Reds and the Chicago White Sox."

"You study it and tell me when I come back."

"Do you think we should buy a lottery ticket with an eighty-five? Tomorrow is the eighty-fifth day."

"We can do that," the boy said. "But what about the eighty-seven of your great record?"

"It could not happen twice. Do you think you can find an eighty-five?"

"I can order one."

"One sheet. That's two dollars and a half. Who can we borrow the money from?"

"That's easy. I can always borrow two dollars and a half."

"I think I can too. But I try not to borrow money. You borrow money at first, but later you will beg.

Keep warm, old man," the boy said. "Remember we are in September."

"The month when the great fish come," the old man said. "Anyone can be a fisherman in May."

"I will go now for the sardines," the boy said.

When the boy came back, the old man was asleep in the chair and the sun had set. The boy took the old army blanket off the bed. He spread it over the back of the chair and over the old man's shoulders. The old man's shoulders were still strong, although they were very old. His neck was still strong too and the wrinkles did not show too much because his head had fallen forward. His shirt had been patched so many times. It was like the sail. The old man's head was very old. With his eyes closed, it looked like there was no life in his face. The newspaper rested on his knees as the evening wind blew. He was barefoot.

Chapter 4
Baseball Game

The boy left him there, and when he came back, the old man was still asleep.

"Wake up old man," the boy said and he put his hand on the old man's knees.

The old man opened his eyes. He had a blank look for a moment, then he smiled.

"What have you got?" he asked.

"Supper," said the boy. "We're going to have supper."

"I'm not very hungry."

"Come on and eat. You can't fish without eating."

"I am used to it," the old man said as he got up, took the newspaper, and folded it. Then he started to fold the blanket.

"Keep the blanket around you," the boy said.

"What are we eating?" the old man said.

"Black beans and rice, fried bananas, and some stew."

The boy had brought them in metal containers from the Terrace. The two sets of knives and forks and spoons were in his pocket with a paper napkin wrapped around each set.

"Who gave this to you?"

"Martin. The owner."

"I must thank him."

"I thanked him already," the boy said. "You don't need

to thank him."

"I'll give him the belly meat of a big fish," the old man said. "Did he give us food before?"

"I think so."

"I must give him something more than the belly meat. He is very thoughtful."

"He sent two beers."

"I like the beer in cans best."

"I know. But this is in bottles. It's Hatuey beer, and I take back the bottles."

"That's very kind of you," the old man said.

"Should we eat?"

"I've been asking you to," the boy told him gently. "I didn't want to open the container until you were ready."

"I'm ready now," the old man said. "I only needed time to wash."

"Where did he wash?" the boy thought.

The village water supply was two streets down the road.

"I should prepare water here for him," the boy thought, "and soap and a good towel. I should get him another shirt, a jacket for the winter, some shoes, and another blanket."

"Your stew is excellent," the old man said.

"Tell me about the baseball game," the boy asked him.

"It is the Yankees in the American League as I said before," the old man said happily.

"They lost today," the boy told him.

"That means nothing. The great DiMaggio is playing well

again."

"They have other men on the team."

"Of course. But he makes the difference. In the other league, between Brooklyn and Philadelphia, I think of Dick Sisler and his great hits in the old baseball park."

"There was nothing ever like his hits. He hits the longest ball I have ever seen."

"Do you remember when he used to come to the Terrace?"

"I wanted to take him fishing but I was too timid to ask him. I asked you to ask him and you were too timid."

"I know. It was a great mistake. He might have gone with us. Then we would have that memory for our whole lives."

"I would like to take the great DiMaggio fishing," the old man said. "People say his father was a fisherman. Maybe he was as poor as we are and maybe he would understand us."

"The great Sisler's father was never poor. He was playing in the Big Leagues when he was my age."

"When I was your age, I was on a ship with a square sail that ran to Africa, and I have seen lions on the beaches in the evening."

"I know. You told me."

"Should we talk about Africa or about baseball?"

"Baseball I think," the boy said. "Tell me about the great John J. McGraw." He said Jota for J.

"He also used to come to the Terrace a long time ago. But he was rough, harsh, and difficult when he was drinking. He thought about horses as well as baseball. He always carried lists of horses in his pocket, and he talked about horses on the telephone many times."

"He was a great manager," the boy said. "My father thinks he was the greatest."

"Because he came here the most times," the old man said. "If Durocher had come here more than McGraw, your father would think he was the greatest manager."

"Who is the greatest manager, really, Luque or Mike Gonzalez?" the boy asked.

"I think they are equal."

"And the best fisherman is you."

"No. I know others who are better."

"No way," the boy said. "I know many good fishermen and I also know some great ones. And then there is only you."

"Thank you. You make me happy. I hope that a big fish does not come along to prove us wrong."

"There is no fish like that if you are strong."

"I may not be as strong as I think," the old man said. "But I know many tricks and I have a strong will."

"You should go to bed now so that you will be fresh in the morning. I will take the things back to the Terrace."

"Good night then. I will wake you in the morning."

"You're my alarm clock," the boy said.

"Age is my alarm clock," the old man said. "Why do old

men wake so early? Is it so that they can have more time during the day?"

"I have no idea," the boy said. "All I know is that young boys sleep in and sleep deeply."

"I can remember it," the old man said. "I'll wake you up in time."

"I don't like it when he wakes me up. It is as if I were beneath him."

"I know."

"Sleep well old man."

"Sleep well."

Chapter 5
Going Fishing

The boy went out. They had eaten at the table without any light. The old man took off his trousers and went to bed in the dark. He rolled his pants up to make a pillow, and he put the newspaper inside his pants. He lay on the bed which was covered with old newspapers. He covered himself with a blanket.

He was asleep in a short time, and he dreamed of when he was a boy in Africa. He dreamed of the long golden beaches, the white beaches, the high capes, and the large brown mountains. He was on the coast every night in his dreams. He heard the waves roar and saw the native boats sailing through them. He smelled the tar and old rope of the deck. He smelled the smell of Africa in the morning breeze.

Usually, when he smelled the breeze, he woke up and got dressed to go and wake up the boy. But tonight, the smell of the breeze came too soon, and he knew it was too early in his dream to wake up. He continued dreaming to see the white peaks of the Islands coming out of the sea. He also dreamed of the different harbors and ports of the Canary Islands.

He no longer dreamed of storms, women, great happenings, great fish, contests of strength, or of his wife. Now he only dreamed of places and the lions on the beach. The lions played like young cats in the sunset and he loved them as he loved the boy. He never dreamed about the boy. He simply woke up, looked out the open door at the moon, and unrolled his trousers and put them on. He relieved himself outside the hut and then went up the road to wake the boy. The morning cold made him shiver, but he knew that he would be warm soon.

The house where the boy lived was unlocked. He opened it and walked in quietly without shoes. The boy was asleep on a folding bed in the first room. The old man could see him clearly in the fading moonlight. He took hold of the boy's foot gently and held it until the boy woke up. The boy turned and looked at him. The old man nodded, and the boy took his trousers from the chair by the bed. The boy sat on the bed and put his pants on. The old man went outside, and the boy came after him. The boy was sleepy. The old man put his arm across his shoulders and said, "I am sorry."

"No, it's alright," the boy said. "It is what a man must do."

They walked down the road to the old man's hut. There were barefoot men moving along the road, carrying the masts of their boats. When they reached the old man's hut, the boy took the rolls of line in the basket, the harpoon, and the gaff. The old man carried the mast with the rolled sail on his shoulder.

"Do you want coffee?" the boy asked.

"We'll put the gear in the boat and then get some."

They drank coffee in condensed milk cans at an early morning coffee shop that served fishermen.

"How did you sleep, old man?" the boy asked.

He was starting to wake up, although he was still sleepy.

"Very well, Manolin," the old man said. "I feel confident today."

"So do I," the boy said. "Now I must get your sardines and mine and your fresh baits. He brings our gear himself. He never wants anyone to carry anything."

"We're different," the old man said. "I let you carry things when you were five years old."

"I know it," the boy said. "I'll be right back. Have another coffee. We already paid for it."

He walked on the coral rocks to the ice house where the baits were stored. The old man drank his coffee slowly. It was the only thing he would have all day, and he knew that he should take it. For a long time now, eating had not interested him and he never brought lunch. He had a bottle of water in the front of the boat, and that was all he needed for the day.

The boy was back now with the sardines and the two baits wrapped in a newspaper. They went down the path to the boat, feeling the pebbles and sand under their feet. They lifted the boat and slid it into the water.

"Good luck, old man."

"Good luck," the old man said.

He fitted the rope of the oars onto the oarlock, and he leaned forward against the movement of the oars in the water. He began to row out of the harbor in the dark. There were other boats from the other harbors going out to sea. The old man heard the push of their oars. The moon was below the hills at that time and he could not see them.

Chapter 6
Bait

Sometimes someone in a boat would speak. But most of the boats were silent except for the push of the oars. They spread apart after they were out of the harbor, and each of them headed for the part of the ocean where they hoped to find fish. The old man determined he was going far out, and he left the smell of the land behind and rowed out into the early morning smell of the ocean.

He saw the glow of the Gulf weed in the water as he rowed over a part of the ocean that the fishermen called "the great well." There was a large hole that was seven hundred fathoms deep. All sorts of fish gathered in the great well, because of the motion the current made on the ocean floor. There were schools of shrimp, baitfish, and sometimes groups of squid in the deepest holes. These fish rose close to the surface at night. The other fish swimming by would eat them.

In the dark, the old man could feel the morning coming. When he rowed away, he heard the trembling sound as flying fish left the water. When they flew away, their hard wings made a hissing sound. They soared away in the darkness. He was very fond of flying fish, as they were his good friends on the ocean.

He was sorry for the birds, especially the small birds, called terns. They were always flying and looking and almost never finding anything. He thought that the birds have a harder life than we do, except for the big birds like robber birds and the heavy, strong birds. Why are those birds so delicate? For those sea swallows, the ocean can be so cruel. The ocean is kind and lovely. But she can be so severe and move so suddenly. Those small birds fly and hunt, singing with their small, sad voices. They are made too delicately for the sea.

He always thought of the sea as "**la mar**", which is what people call her in Spanish when they love her. Even those who love the sea sometimes say bad things about her. They always speak as though the sea was a woman. Some younger fishermen made a lot of money from shark livers. They had motorboats and used buoys. They spoke of the sea as "**el mar**", which is masculine. They spoke of her as a competitor, a place, or even an enemy. But the old man always thought of her as feminine. He thought of her as something that gave things or took things away from people. If she did wild or wicked things, it was because she could not help people. He thought that the moon would affect the sea, like the moon would affect a woman.

He was rowing steadily and it was no effort for him. He kept well within his speed and the surface of the ocean was flat, except for the occasional movements of the current. He was letting the current do one third of the work for him. The light was coming. He saw he was already further out than he had hoped to be at this hour.

"I worked the deep wells for one week and did nothing," he thought. "Today I'll go out where the schools of bonito are. Maybe there will be a big fish there with them.

Before it was light, he had his baits out and he was drifting with the current. One bait was down forty fathoms. The second was at seventy-five fathoms, and the third and fourth were down in the blue water at one hundred and one hundred twenty-five fathoms. Each bait hung head down with the long part of the hook inside the baitfish. They were tied and sewed in place. The projecting part of the hook — the curve and the point — was covered with fresh sardines. Each sardine was hooked through both eyes so that they made a half-loop on the outside steel. Every part of the hook would be sweet smelling and good tasting to a big fish.

The boy had given him two fresh small tunas called albacores, which hung on the two deepest fishing lines. He also had a big blue runner and a yellow jack hung on the others. They had been used before. However, they were still in good condition. There were also excellent sardines that smelled good and looked good. Each fishing line was as thick around as a big pencil. Each of them were looped onto a green float stick so that any pull or touch on the bait would make the stick dip down in the water. Each line had two forty-fathom spools that could be connected fast to the other spare spools so that a fish could take out over three hundred fathoms of line.

Now the man watched the dip of the three sticks over the side of the boat. He rowed gently to keep the lines straight up and down and at their proper depths. It would soon be light, and the sun would rise any moment now. The sun rose gently from the sea, and the old man could see the other boats. The other boats were low on the water and near the coast, spread out across the current. Then the sun was brighter, and the glare came on the water. The sun rose brightly. The flat sea reflected the sunshine back on his eyes. This hurt his eyes badly, and he rowed without looking into the sun.

He looked down into the water and watched the lines that went straight down into the water's darkness. He kept the lines straighter than anyone did, so that at each bait would rest at each level in the darkness. Each bait would be exactly where he wanted it to be. Others let the lines drift with the current. Sometimes the lines were at sixty fathoms when the fishermen thought they were at a hundred.

But he thought, "I keep them in the right place. Only I have no luck anymore. But who knows? Maybe today is the day. Every day is a new day. It is better to be lucky. But I would rather be exact. Then when luck comes, you are ready."

Chapter 7
A Man-Of-War Bird

The sun was now two hours higher, and it did not hurt his eyes to look to the east. There were only three boats in sight and they had come very low and far inshore.

He thought, "All my life the early morning sun has hurt my eyes. Yet my eyes are still good. In the evening I can look straight into the light without getting the blackness. The light is stronger in the evening. But in the morning it is painful."

Just then, he saw a man-of-war bird with his long black wings flying circles in the sky. The bird made a quick drop, moving downward on with his wings pushed back, and the bird flew in a circle again.

"He's got something," the old man said aloud. "He's not just looking."

He rowed slowly and steadily toward where the bird was circling. He did not hurry and he kept his lines straight up and down. But he touched the current a little so that he was still fishing correctly even though he fished at a faster speed than normal.

The bird went higher in the air and circled again, his wings did not move. Then he dove suddenly and the old man saw flying fish. The flying fish shot out of the water and sailed quickly over the water's surface.

"Dolphin," the old man said aloud. "Big dolphin."

He stopped rowing, put his oars away, and brought a small line from under the bow. It had a wire leader and a medium-sized hook. He baited it with one of the sardines. He let it go over the side and then attached it to the back of the boat. Then he baited another line and left it coiled in the bow. He went back to rowing and watched the blackbird who was flying low over the water.

As he watched, the bird dipped down again and bent its wings for the dive. The bird followed the flying fish, swinging its wings wildly. The old man could see the big lump coming out of the water as the dolphin followed the flying fish. The dolphin was cutting through the water beneath the fish as it flew. The dolphin swam at top speed to catch the flying fish when the fish dropped.

"It is a big school of dolphins," he thought. "They are scattered and the flying fish have no chance to escape. The bird has no chance to get them. The flying fish are too big for him and they go too fast."

He watched the flying fish burst out of the water again and again he saw the bird move without success.

"That school of dolphin got away from me," he thought. "They are moving out too quickly and going far away. But perhaps I will pick up a lone fish and maybe my big fish will be around them. My big fish must be somewhere."

Now, the clouds over the land rose up like mountains. The coast was only a long green line with the gray and blue hills behind it. The water was so dark blue, it was almost a purple color. As he looked down into it, he saw the red sifting of the plankton in the dark water. Strange light shown down from the sun. He watched his lines to see them go straight down. He was happy to see so much plankton, because it meant there were fish nearby.

The sun continued to shine the strange light on the water. The sun was higher. This meant good weather, and so did the shape of the clouds over the land. But the bird was almost out of sight and nothing could be seen on the surface of the water. There were some patches of yellow Sargasso weed and the bladder of a purple jellyfish, called a Portuguese man-of-war. The body of the jellyfish began to shimmer as it took shape and floated beside the boat. It turned on its side and then turned back over. It floated happily like a bubble, it's long, purple tentacles stretching out for one meter behind it in the water.

"*Agua mala*," the man said. "You trickster."

He looked down into the water while he swung his oars lightly. He saw the tiny fish that were swimming between the Portuguese man-of-war. They were the same color as the jellyfish. The jellyfish made shadows as they moved. The tiny fish were immune to its poison. But humans were not immune to its poison. Sometimes, these jellyfish would stick to a line. They would cause blisters and pain on the old man's hands, just like poison ivy. But the poison from the "**agua mala**" came quickly and caused people more pain.

The rainbow-colored bubbles were beautiful. But jellyfish were the most deceiving thing in the sea. The old man loved to see the giant sea turtles eating the jellyfish. When the turtles saw them, they approached them from the front. The turtles ate them all while covering their body in their shell. The old man loved to see the turtles eat them. He also loved to walk on them on the beach after a storm. He loved to hear them "pop" when he stepped on them with the firm bottoms of his feet.

He loved green turtles and hawk-bills with their elegance, speed, and great value. He had a playful bitterness towards the huge, stupid loggerheads. They were yellow in their ar-mor-plating, strange in their breeding style, and happy to eat the Portuguese men-of-war with their eyes shut.

He had no fantasies about turtles although he had gone in turtle boats for many years. He was sorry for the turtles, even the turtles with large trunk backs. Those turtles were as long as the boat and they were very heavy. Most people do not care at all about turtles because a turtle's heart will continue to beat, even after the turtle was caught, killed, and cut up.

But the old man thought, "I have a heart too. My feet and hands are like theirs."

He ate the white turtle eggs to give himself strength. He ate them all through the month of May to be strong in September and October to catch the giant fish.

He also drank a cup of shark liver oil each day from the big drum. It was free for all fishermen. Most fishermen hated the taste. But it was no worse than getting up early in the morning. And it was very good to treat colds and the flu. It was also good for the eyes.

Chapter 8
Albacore

Now the old man looked up and saw that the bird was circling again.

"He found some fish," he said aloud.

No flying came through the surface of the water and there was no spreading out of bait fish. But while the old man watched, a small tuna rose in the air and dropped head first into the water. The tuna was shining with a silver color in the sunlight, and after he had dropped back into the water, more tuna jumped up in the air. They were jumping in all directions, stirring the water and chasing the bait. They were swimming in circles around the bait.

"If they don't move too fast, I will sail into this group of fish," the old man thought.

He watched the school of tuna turning the water white and the bird now flying down and diving into the bait fish that swam to the surface in fear.

"The bird is a great help," the old man said.

Just then the back of the boat fishing line became tight under his foot, where he had kept a loop of the line. He dropped his oars and held the line firm. He started to bring the fish into the boat. He felt the weight of the small tuna as it shook. The shaking increased as he pulled in the boat. He could see the blue back and the gold sides of the fish in the water. He swung it over the side and into the boat. The tuna lay in the back of the boat in the sun. The tuna was small and shaped like a bullet. The tuna's big eyes were staring at the old man. The tuna thumped its body against the boat with its tail moving fast. The old man kindly hit the tuna on the head and kicked it, knocking it out. The tuna's body was still shaking in the shade in the back of the boat.

"Albacore," he said out loud. "It will make a beautiful bait. It will weigh ten pounds."

He did not remember when he started to speak out loud to himself. A long time ago, he sang songs at night when he was alone in the fishing boats.

He had probably started to talk out loud when the boy had left. But he did not remember. When he and the boy fished together, they usually spoke only when they needed to. They talked at night or when they couldn't go fishing because of bad weather. It was considered a good thing not to have "small talk" out on the ocean. The old man had always considered this. Now he said his thoughts out loud.

"If the others heard me talking loudly, they would think that I am crazy," he said out loud. "But since I am not crazy, I do not care. And the rich men have radios to talk to them in their boats and also to bring them the baseball news."

"Now is not the time to think of baseball," he thought. "Now is the time to think of just one thing. That is fishing.

There might be a big fish around here. I just picked up the albacore that was left behind. But they are quickly moving far out. Everything on the surface of the water is moving very fast and to the northeast. Is it the time of day for this? Or is it some signal in the weather that I do not know about?"

He could not see the green of the shore. He could see the tops of the blue hills that showed snow-capped and the clouds that looked like high mountains. The sea was very dark and the light made prisms in the water. A lot of the plankton died off now in the sunlight, and the old man could only see the great deep prisms in the water. His fishing lines went straight down into the water.

Chapter 9
Encounter

The tunas were down again. The fishermen called all the fish of that species 'tuna'. The fishermen only separated them into their proper names when they came to sell them or to trade them for baits. The sun was hot now, and the old man felt it on the back of his neck and felt the sweat run slowly down his back as he rowed.

"I could drift," he thought, "and I could sleep and put a loop of line around my toe to wake me. But today is eighty-five days, and I should fish well today."

Just then, he saw one of the floating green sticks dip sharply.

"Yes," he said. "Yes," and put his oars inside the boat without hitting it.

He reached out for the line and held it softly between the thumb and index finger of his right hand. He did not feel strain or weight. He held onto the line lightly. Then he felt the pulling of the line. This time it was a light pull; it was not solid or heavy, and he knew exactly what it was. One hundred fathoms down, a marlin was eating the sardines that covered the point and the shank of the hook.

The old man held the line delicately and softly as he untied it from the stick with his left hand. Now he could let it move through his fingers without the fish feeling any tension.

"Since he is this far out, he must be huge in this season," he thought. "Eat them, fish. Eat them. Please eat them. They are so fresh and you are down there six hundred feet in that cold water in the dark. Turn around in the dark and come back and eat them."

He felt the light, gentle pulling and then a harder pull when a sardine's head must have been more difficult to break from the hook. Then there was nothing.

"Come on," the old man said out loud. "Turn back around. Just smell them. Aren't they lovely? Eat well, and then you can have the tuna. It's hard, cold, and lovely. Don't be shy, fish. Eat them."

He waited with the line between his thumb and his

finger. He watched it and the other lines at the same time, because the fish might have swum up or down. Then he felt the same gentle pulling touch again.

"The fish will take it," the old man said out loud. "God, help it to take the bait."

But it did not take it. It was gone and the old man felt nothing.

"It couldn't have gone," he said. "Heaven only knows... it couldn't have gone away. It's turning around. Maybe it has been hooked before and it remembers that experience."

Then he felt the gentle touch on the line and he was happy.

"It just turned around," he said. "It'll take it."

He was happy feeling the gentle pulling. But then, he felt something. It was hard and extremely heavy. It was the weight of the fish. The man let the line slip down, down, down. He unrolled the first of the two reserve coils. The fishing line went down, slipping lightly through the old man's fingers. He still felt the huge weight, but he could not really feel the pressure between his fingers.

"What a fish," he said. "It has the bait sideways in his mouth now and it is leaving with it."

"Then the fish will turn and swallow it," he thought.

He did not say that because he knew that if he spoke, it might not happen. He knew what a giant fish this was and he thought of the fish swimming away with the tuna in its mouth. At that moment, he felt the fish stop moving, but the weight was still there. Then the weight increased and he released more line. He tightened pressure between his fingers and the weight increased. It was going straight down.

"The fish took it," he said. "Now, I'll let the fish enjoy it."

He let the line slip through his fingers. He reached down with his left hand and connected the two extra lines to the spool of the next line. Now he was ready. He had three forty-fathom spools of extra line.

"Eat it a little more," he said. "Eat it all."

"Eat it so that the point of the hook goes into your heart and kills you," he thought. "Come up quickly and let me put the harpoon into you. All right. Are you ready? Have you been eating for long enough?"

"Now!" he said out loud and pulled the line hard with both hands. He got another yard of line and pulled again, with each of his arms taking a turn pulling the line with all his strength.

Nothing happened. The fish just moved slowly away and the old man could not bring the fish up one inch. His line was strong and made for heavy fish. He held it against his back until it was so tight that drops of water were dripping from it. Then the line made a slow hissing sound in the water. The man still held it. He supported himself against the boat and leaned back against the pressure of the line. The boat began to move slowly toward the northwest.

The fish moved along. The boat traveled slowly on the calm water. The other baits were still in the water, but the man could not do anything.

"I wish I had the boy here," the old man said out loud. "I'm being pulled by the fish and I'm the towing peg. I could fasten the line to the boat, but then the fish could break it. I must hold on for as long as I can, and give the fish more line when he wants some. Thank God, the fish is moving forward and not going down."

"What will I do if he decides to go down?" he thought. "I don't know. What will I do if he goes down and dies? I don't know. But I'll do something. There are a lot of things I could do."

He held the line against his back and watched the line in the water. The boat was moving steadily to the northwest.

"This will kill him," the old man thought. "The fish can't do this forever."

But the fish was still swimming steadily. For the next four hours, the fish pulled the boat. The old man was still supported firmly with the line across his back.

"It was noon when I hooked the fish," he said. "And I haven't even seen it yet."

He pushed his hat down roughly on his head before he hooked the fish. This hurt his forehead. He was thirsty too. He got down on his knees. He was careful not to move the line. He moved as far into the front of the boat as he could go and reached the water bottle with one hand. He opened it and drank a little. Then he rested against the front of the boat. He tried not to think too much. He decided to just keep going.

Then he looked behind him and the land was no longer visible.

"That makes no difference," he thought. "I can always come back home by the light from Havana. There are two more hours before the sun sets. Maybe the fish will come up before that. If it doesn't, maybe it will come up with the moon. If it does not do that, maybe it will come up with the sunrise. I have no muscle pain and I feel strong. The fish is the one who has the hook in his mouth. But what a strong fish to pull a boat like that. The fish must be biting the wire. I wish I could see it. I wish I could see it only once so I could know what kind of fish I'm fighting."

Chapter 10
Moving Along

The fish did not change its direction for a whole night. The man could tell from watching the stars. It was cold after the sun went down, and the old man's sweat dried cold on his body. He took the sack that covered the bait box. He dried the sack earlier that day. After the sun went down, he tied it around his neck. The sack hung down over his back. He carefully worked it down under the line that was across his shoulders. The sack cushioned the line, and he had found a way of leaning forward against the bow. The position was only somewhat less painful. But he thought it was almost comfortable.

"As long as the fish continues this, I can do nothing with the fish and the fish can do nothing with me," he thought.

At that moment he stood up and relieved himself over the side of the boat. He looked at the stars and checked his course. The line was like a bright stripe in the water straight out from his shoulders. They were moving more slowly now, and the light from Havana was not so strong. He knew that the current must be carrying them to the east.

"If I lose the light of Havana, we must be going more towards the east," he thought. "If the fish keeps going like this, I will have to look at it for a long time."

"I wonder how the baseball game turned out in the big leagues today," he thought. "It would be wonderful to do this with a radio."

Then he thought, "think of this always. Think of what you are doing. You must not be stupid."

Then he said out loud, "I wish I had the boy here. I wish he could help me and see this."

"People in their old age shouldn't be alone," he thought.

"But I have no choice. I must remember to eat the tuna before it goes bad. I need to keep strong. Remember that you must eat tuna in the morning. Remember..." He said to himself.

Two porpoises came around the boat during the night, and he could hear them rolling and puffing. He could tell the difference between the puffing noise the male made and the puffing noise the female made.

"They are good," he said. "They play, make jokes, and love one another. They are our brothers like the flying fish."

Then he began to feel bad for the great fish that he had hooked.

"The fish is wonderful and strange. Who knows how old it is," he thought. "I have never had such a strong fish. The fish is acting in an interesting way. Perhaps the fish is too wise to jump. It could break me by jumping or rushing away wildly. But maybe the fish has been hooked many times before. The fish knows how to fight. The fish cannot know that there is only one old man hooking it. But this is a great fish. If the meat is good, I will get a good price for it in the market. The fish bit the bait like a male, and pulls it like a male does. The fish does not have any panic. I wonder if it has any plans. Or is the fish just as desperate as I am?"

He remembered the time he had caught one of a pair of marlin. The male fish let the female fish eat the feed first. So he hooked the female fish. The female got in a panic and she started to fight. She got exhausted. But the male had stayed with her that whole time. The male fish swam across the fishing line and swam in a circle on the surface of the water. He had stayed so close that the old man was afraid the marlin would cut the line with his tail. The marlin's tail was sharp as a knife.

The old man held the blade skin with its sandpaper edge and hit her across the top of her head. When the old man had clubbed the female fish, the male fish had stayed by the side of the boat. The old man hit the female fish until her color changed and looked like the back of a mirror. Then the old man lifted the fish onto the boat. The male fish still stayed by the boat. The old man was clearing the lines and preparing the harpoon. Just then, the male fish jumped high into the air beside the boat to see where the female fish was. Then the male fish went down into the water. His lavender wings that were his inner fins spread out wide and all his wide lavender stripes were showing.

"He was beautiful," the old man remembered, "and he had stayed."

"That was the saddest thing I ever saw with them," the old man thought. "The boy was sad too, and we said we were sorry and killed her quickly."

"I wish the boy were here," he said out loud.

He settled himself against the planks of the bow. He felt the strength of the big fish through the line he held across his shoulders. The boat was moving toward wherever the fish was going.

"When once it had been necessary for him to make a choice," the old man thought. "His choice had been to stay in the deep dark water far out beyond all traps and tricks. My choice was to go there to find him beyond all people. Now we are joined together and have been since noon. And no one to help either one of us. Perhaps I should not have been a fisherman. But I was born to be a fisherman. I must surely remember to eat the tuna after it gets light."

Chapter 11
Tug-of-War

Sometime before daylight, something took one of the baits. He heard the stick break and the line begin to unravel over the edge of the boat. In the darkness, he loosened his knife and held the tight weight of the fish's line on his left shoulder. He leaned back and cut the line against the wood on the side of the boat. Then he cut the other line closest to him. He tied the loose ends of the extra coils together in the dark. He worked with skill and used only one hand, as he put his foot on the coils to hold them. Now he had six extra coils of line. There were two from each bait and the two from the bait the fish had taken. They were all tied together.

"After sunrise, I will work back to the back of the boat. I will cut the rest of the line and link up the extra coils," he thought. "I will have lost 360 meters of the good quality line, the hooks, and main fishing lines. That can be replaced. But if I hook some fish and it cuts him off, who replaces this big fish? I don't know what that fish was. It could have been a marlin or a broadbill or a shark. I never felt him. I had to get rid of him too fast."

He said out loud, "I wish I had the boy."

"But you haven't got the boy," he thought. "You only have yourself. You had better work back to the last line now. You need to cut it away, and you need to hook up the two extra spools — in the dark or not in the dark."

So he did it. It was difficult in the dark. Once, the fish made a wave that pulled him down on his face and made a cut below his eye. The blood ran down onto part of his cheek, but the blood dried before it came to his chin. He worked his way back to the front of the boat and rested against the wood.

He adjusted the sack. He carefully moved the line so that it came across a new part of his shoulders. He held it tightly with his shoulders. He carefully felt the fish and felt the speed of the boat with his hand.

"I wonder why he swerved like that," he thought. "The wire must have slipped on the fish's back. His back must not feel as badly as mine feels. He cannot pull this boat forever, no matter how great he is. Now there is no problem and everything is cleared away. And I have some extra fishing line. This is all I have."

"Fish," he said softly. "I'll stay with you until I am dead."

"The fish will stay with me too, I guess," the old man thought.

He waited for it to be light. It was cold now in the time before daylight, and he pushed against the wood to be warm.

"I can do it as long as the fish can," he thought.

And in the first light, the line stretched out and went

down into the water. The boat continued to move. When the sun started to rise, the line was on the old man's right shoulder.

"He's headed north," the old man said.

"The current will have set us far to the eastward," he thought. "I wish he would turn with the current. That means he would be getting tired."

When the sun had risen further, the old man realized that the fish was not getting tired. There was only one positive sign. The direction of the line showed he was swimming at a more shallow depth. That did not exactly mean that the fish would jump. But the fish might.

"God, let him jump," the old man said. "I have enough line to handle him."

"Maybe if I can tighten the line, it will hurt him, and he will jump," he thought. "Let him jump. The fish will fill the sacks in his back with air, and then it cannot go deep to die."

He tried to increase the tension, but the line had been tightly stretched up to the breaking point. He felt the stiff line as he leaned back to pull on it. He knew that he could put no more strain on it.

"I must not yank it ever," he thought. "Each yank widens the cut that the hook makes, and then when he does jump, he might throw it. Anyway, I feel better about where the sun is now. Finally, I do not have to look into it."

There was yellow weed on the line, but the old man was pleased. He knew that only made an added burden. It was the yellow Gulf weed that shone with a glowing light in the night.

"Fish," he said, "I love you and respect you very much. But I will kill you before this day ends. Let us hope so", he thought.

Chapter 12
A small Bird

A small bird came toward the boat from the north. The bird was a warbler and it was flying very low over the water. The old man could see that the bird was very tired. The bird sat at the stern of the boat and rested there. Then he flew around the old man's head and rested on the line. The bird was more comfortable there.

"How old are you?" the old man asked the bird. "Is this your first trip?"

When he spoke, the bird looked at him. The bird was too tired to even look at the line. The bird wobbled on the line as its feet gripped it tightly.

"It's steady," the old man told him. "It's too steady. Last night there was no wind. Why are you so tired? What's happening with birds these days?"

"The hawks come out to sea to meet these little birds," he thought.

But he didn't say anything about this to the bird, since the bird could not understand him anyway. The bird would learn about the hawks soon.

"Take a good rest, small bird," he said. "Then go ahead and take your chance like any man or bird or fish."

He was happy to talk to someone because his back was really hurting now.

"Stay at my house if you want, bird," he said. "I am sorry I cannot raise the sail and take you in with the small breeze. But I am with a friend."

The fish suddenly moved and it pulled the old man down onto the bow of the boat. The fish almost pulled him overboard, but he gave the fish some extra line. The bird flew up when the line was yanked, and the old man did not even see the bird leave.

He felt the line carefully with his right hand and noticed his hand was bleeding.

"So, something hurt the fish," he said out loud.

He pulled back on the line to see if he could turn the fish over. But when he was touching the weak part of the line, he held on and leaned back on the tight part of the line.

"You're feeling it now, fish," he said. "And so am I."

He looked around for the bird because he would have

liked to have the bird there for company. The bird was gone.

"You did not stay long," the man thought. "But it is tough where you are going, until you get to the shore."

"How did I let the fish make me fall with one quick pull? I must be getting foolish. Or maybe I was looking at the small bird and thinking of him," he thought. "Now I will focus on my work. I must eat the tuna, so I will not lose more strength."

"I wish the boy were here and that I had some salt," he said out loud.

Chapter 13
Left Hand

He moved the weight of the line to his left shoulder. He knelt carefully and washed his hand in the ocean. He kept his hand there for more than a minute. He watched the blood trail away. He watched the steady movement of the water against his hand as the boat moved.

"He is moving much slowly now," he said.

The old man would have liked to keep his hand in the saltwater longer, but he was afraid that the fish might move suddenly again. He stood up and steadied himself. He held his hand up to the light of the sun. The hand injury was only a line burn that had cut his skin. But this burn was in the working part of his hand.He knew he would need both of his hands for work and he did not like being hurt before the busy work started.

"Now," when his hand had dried, he said. "I must eat the small tuna. I can reach him with the gaff and eat him here,"

He knelt and found the tuna under the front part of the boat. He used his gaff to pull the tuna towards himself. He kept it away from the fishing lines. Holding the line with his left shoulder and keeping his left arm steady, he took the tuna off the gaff hook and put the gaff away. He put one knee on the fish and cut it into strips. He cut the meat vertically. He cut the pieces of fish into wedges, from the tuna's backbone to its belly. When he had cut six strips, he spread them out on the wood of the bow. He wiped his knife on his trousers, lifted the tuna's remains by the tail, and dropped it overboard.

"I don't think I can eat a whole piece," he said.

He dragged his knife across one of the strips of tuna. He could feel the tightness of the line, and a cramp in his left hand. He pulled up his stiff hand on the heavy cord. He looked at it and felt sickened.

"What kind of a hand is that," he said. "Go ahead. Stop moving if you want... Make yourself into a claw. It will not help you."

He looked down into the dark water at the direction of the line.

"Eat it now, and it will strengthen your hand. It is not the hand's fault, and you have been out here for so long with the fish. Eat the tuna now," he thought.

He picked up a piece and put it in his mouth. He chewed it slowly. It was not unpleasant.

"Chew it well," he thought, "And get all the juices. This would be good to eat with a little lime, lemon, or salt."

"How do you feel, hand?" he asked this to his cramped hand that was almost as stiff as the hand of a dead person. "I'll eat some more for you."

He ate the other part of the piece of fish he had cut in

two. He chewed it carefully and then spat out the skin.

"How is it going, hand? Or is it too early to tell?" He ate another full piece.

"It is a strong, wholesome fish," he thought. "I was lucky to get him instead of catching a dolphin. Dolphin meat is too sweet. This tuna is not sweet, and it's still strong."

"There is no need to be fancy now. I need to be practical," he thought. "I wish I had some salt. I don't know if the fish will dry in the sun or if it will spoil. I should eat it all, even though I'm not hungry. The fish is calm and steady. I will eat all of the tuna, and then I'll be ready."

"Be patient, hand," he said. "I am doing this for you."

"I wish I could feed the fish," he thought. "He is my brother. But I must kill him."

He ate all of the wedge-shaped strips of fish slowly and carefully. He straightened up and wiped his hand on his trousers.

"Now," he said. "Hand, you can let the line go. I will handle it with my right arm until you stop acting this way."

He put his left foot on the heavy line and lay back against the tight part of the line on his back.

"God, help my hand to be released from this cramp," he said. "I do not know what the fish is going to do."

"But he seems calm," he thought. "The fish is following

his plan. But what is his plan? What is my plan? My plan depends on his plan, because of his great size. If he jumps, I can kill him. But he is staying down there forever. Then I will stay down with him forever."

He rubbed the cramped hand against his trousers. He tried to open his fingers. But they would not open.

"Maybe my hand will open with the sun," he thought. "Maybe it will open when the healthy tuna is digested. If I have to use my hand, I will force it to open, whatever it costs. But I do not want to open it now by force. I will let it open by itself and come back naturally. I misused it in the night when I needed it to free and untie the fishing lines."

Chapter 14
Jumping Up

He looked across the sea and knew how alone he was. But he could see the prisms in the deep, dark water. He saw the fishing line stretching out and the ocean water moving smoothly, up and down. The clouds were building up now to prepare for the northeast winds. He looked forward and saw a flight of wild ducks. The wild ducks flew high above the water and their shapes stretched out over the sky. Their outlines became blurry, then they came into focus again. He knew no man was ever alone on the sea.

"Some men are afraid of being out of the sight of land in a small boat," he thought. "They are right in the seasons of bad weather. But now it's hurricane season. If there are no hurricanes, the weather is really very nice."

If there is a hurricane coming, you always see the signs of it in the sky at sea. People do not see it on the land because they do not know what to look for, he thought. The land also affects the shape of the clouds. But we have no hurricane coming now.

He looked at the sky. He saw the white cumulus clouds stacked like friendly piles of ice cream. He also saw the thin streaks of cirrus clouds high in the September sky.

"A light *brisa*," he said. "Better weather for me than for

you, fish."

His left hand was still cramped, but it was slowly becoming more relaxed.

"I hate cramps. They are a betrayal of one's own body," he thought. "It is a shameful thing in front of others to have diarrhea from food poisoning. But a cramp is an embarrassment to oneself, especially when one is alone."

"If the boy were here, he could rub it for me and make the muscle relax," he thought. "But the cramp will go later on."

Then, with his right hand, he felt the difference in the fishing line. He saw the direction of the line change in the water. He leaned against the line and slapped his left hand hard against his leg. He saw the line tilt upward.

"He's coming up," he said. "Come on hand. Please move."

The line rose slowly. Then the surface of the ocean bubbled up in front of the boat and the fish came out. He came out continuously, and water poured from his sides. He was bright in the sun, and his head and back were dark purple. The stripes on his sides showed a light lavender color. His sword was as long as a baseball bat and the tip was as sharp as a sword. He jumped from the water and then re-entered it, smoothly, like a diver. The old man saw the great blade of his tail go into the water. The line went quickly into the sea again.

"He is two feet longer than the boat," the old man said.

The line was going out fast but steadily. The fish was not afraid. The old man was trying to hold the line with both hands so that it wouldn't break. He knew that if he could not make the fish slow down, the fish could take out all the line and break it.

"He is a great fish, and I must trick him," he thought. "I must never let him learn how strong he is, or what he could do if he escapes from me. If I were him, I would try with all my energy and swim away until the fishing line broke. Thank God, fish are not as smart as the people who kill them, even though they are more powerful."

The old man had seen many great fish. He had seen many that weighed more than a thousand pounds. He had caught two of that size in his life, but never alone. Now he was holding on to catch the biggest fish that he had ever seen. But He was alone, and his left hand was still as tight as the claws of an eagle.

"It will uncramp though," he thought. "Surely it will uncramp to help my right hand. Three things are like brothers: the fish and my two hands. My hand must uncramp."

The fish slowed again and was going at his usual pace.

"I wonder why he jumped," the old man thought.

"Maybe he jumped to show me how big he was. Well, now, I know," he thought. "I wish I could show him what sort of man I am. But then he would see my cramped hand. Let him think I am stronger than I really am and I will be stronger."

"I wish I was the fish," he thought. The fish has everything. All I have against him is my will and my intelligence.

Chapter 15
The Prayer

He settled comfortably against the boat and endured his difficulties. The fish continued to swim, and the boat moved slowly through the dark water. There was a small sea rising with the wind coming up from the east. The cramp was gone from the old man's left hand at noon.

"Bad news for you, fish," he said. He moved the line over the sacks that covered his shoulders. He was comfortable but suffering, although he did not admit that he was suffering at all.

"I am not religious," he said. "But I will pray ten Our Fathers and ten Ave Maria prayers so that I can catch this fish. If I catch him, I promise to go to visit the statue of the Virgin of Cobre. That is a promise."

He began to say his prayers mechanically. Sometimes he would be so tired that he could not remember the prayer. Then, he would say the prayers fast, so that they would come out automatically.

"Ave Marias are easier to say than Our Fathers," he thought.

"Ave Maria full of Grace the Lord is with thee. Blessed art thou among women and blessed is the fruit of thy womb, Jesus. Holy Mary, Mother of God, pray for us sinners, now and at the hour of our death. Amen."

Then he added, "Blessed Mary, pray for the death of this fish."

He was feeling much better with his prayers, but he was suffering just as much. He leaned against the front of the boat. He began to stretch the fingers of his left hand mechanically. The sun was hot now, although the breeze was rising gently.

"I had better re-bait that little line out over the back of the boat," he said. "If the fish decides to stay another night, I will need to eat again, and the water is low in the bottle. I think I can only get a dolphin here. But if I eat him fresh enough, he won't be bad. I wish a flying fish would jump onto the boat tonight. But I have no light to attract them. A flying fish is wonderful to eat raw, and I would not have to cut him up. I must save all my strength now. Oh my, I did not know he was so big."

"Anyway, I'll kill him," he said. "In all his greatness and his glory." Although it is not fair, he thought. "I will show him what a man can do and what a man endures."

"I told the boy that I was a strange old man," he said. "Now I must prove it."

He had proved it a thousand times, but that meant nothing. Now he was proving it again. Each time was a new time, and he never thought about the past. He just did it again.

"I wish he would sleep, and I could sleep and dream about the lions," he thought.

"Why do lions always appear in dreams? Don't think, old man," he said to himself, "Now rest gently against the boat and don't think too hard. The fish is still working. Don't work so hard."

The morning was changing to afternoon, and the boat still moved slowly and steadily. But there was an added drag now from the easterly breeze. The old man rode gently with the small waves, and pain across his back from the cord felt easier to handle.

Once in the afternoon, the line started to rise again. But the fish only continued to swim a little bit upwards. The sun was on the old man's left arm, shoulder, and his back. So he knew the fish had turned to the east from the north.

He had seen the fish once. He could picture the fish swimming in the water with his purple inner fins spread out as wide as wings, and the great, tall tail zipping through the darkness. "I wonder how much he sees at that depth," the old man thought. "His eye is huge, and a horse has smaller eyes, and it can still see in the dark. Once I could see quite well in the dark. I could not see in complete darkness, but my eyesight was like a cat."

The sun and the steady movement of his fingers had uncramped his left hand. He began to shift more of the pressure to his left hand. He shrugged the muscles of his back to shift the pain of the line a little.

"If you're not tired, fish," he said out loud, "you must be very strange."

He felt very tired and he knew the night would come soon. He tried to think of other things. He thought of Major League Baseball. It's called the "**Gran Ligas**" in Spanish. He knew that the New York Yankees were playing the Detroit Tigers.

"It's the second day now and I do not know the result of the games," he thought. "But I must have confidence. I must be worthy of the great DiMaggio. He does all things perfectly, even with the pain of the bone spur in his heel."

"What is a bone spur?" he asked himself. "We call it "**Un espuela de hueso**," in Spanish. We do not have them. Can it be as painful as the spur of a fighting rooster in one's heel? I do not think I could endure that. I could not endure the loss of an eye or even both eyes and continue fighting as the fighting roosters do either. Humans are really not much beside the great birds and other animals. Still, I would rather be that animal down there in the darkness of the sea."

"Unless sharks come," he said out loud. "If sharks come, God, pity him and me."

"Do you think the great DiMaggio would stay with a fish for as long as I will stay with this one?" he thought. "I am sure he would stay and for even longer since he is young and strong. Also, his father was a fisherman. But would the bone spur hurt him too much?"

"I do not know," he said out loud. "I have never had a bone spur."

Chapter 16
Arm Wrestling

As the sun set, he wanted to give himself confidence. He remembered the time in the bar at Casablanca, when he arm-wrestled with the great black man from Cienfuegos. The black man was the strongest man on the docks.

They had played one day and one night with their elbows on a chalk line on the table. Their forearms were straight up, and their hands gripped each other tight. Each one was trying to force the other's hand down onto the table. Many people were betting money, and people went in and out of the room under the lamp lights. He looked at the black man's arm, hand, and face.

There were referees at the wrestling game. They changed referees every four hours after the first eight hours. They needed to sleep. Blood came out from under the fingernails of both of their hands. They looked at each other in the eye, and they looked at their hands and forearms. The bettors went in and out of the room and sat on high chairs against the wall and watched. The wooden walls were painted bright blue. The lamps threw their shadows against the walls. The black man's shadow was huge, and it moved on the wall as the breeze moved the lamps.

The odds would change back and forth all night. People

fed the black man rum and lighted cigarettes for him. After the rum, the black man would give his very best effort. Once, he had the old man—who was not an old man then, but was Santiago **El Campeon**—nearly three inches off balance. But the old man had raised his hand up, even again. He was sure that he had the black man, who was a great athlete, beaten.

At daylight, the bettors were asking that the game be called off as a draw. The referee was shaking his head. He had suddenly exerted his effort and forced the hand of the black man down until it touched the wood.

The game had started on a Sunday morning and ended on a Monday morning. Many of the bettors had asked for a draw because they had to work on the docks. They loaded sacks of sugar or worked at the Havana Coal Company. Otherwise, everyone would have wanted the game to go on until it finished. But the old man had finished it anyway and it was done before anyone had to go to work.

For a long time after that, everyone had called him "The Champion." There had been a return game in the spring. But not much money was bet. He had won it quite easily since he had broken the black man's confidence.

After that, he played a few games and then stopped. He could beat anyone if he really wanted to. He decided playing games was bad for his right hand for fishing. He tried a few practice games with his left hand. But his left hand had always let him down. The left hand would not do what he told it to do, so he did not trust his left hand.

"The sun will keep it warm now," he thought. "It won't get cramped again unless it gets too cold in the night. I wonder what will happen tonight."

An airplane passed overhead on its way to Miami. He watched its shadow scaring up the schools of flying fish.
"With so much flying fish, there should be some dolphins too," he said.
He leaned back on the line to see if it was possible to come nearer to his fish. But he could not. It stayed at the tight part of the fishing line where the water was swirling and shivering. The boat moved ahead slowly. He watched the airplane until he could no longer see it.

"It must be very strange in an airplane," he thought. "I

wonder what the sea looks like from that height? They should be able to see the fish well if they do not fly too high. I would like to fly in the sky at two hundred fathoms and see the fish from above."

When I was on the turtle boats, I was on the masthead's cross-trees. Even at that height, I saw so many things. The dolphins look greener from there. You can see their stripes and purple spots. You can see the whole school of dolphins as they swim. Why is it that all of the fast-moving fish have purple backs and usually purple stripes or spots? The dolphin looks green because he is golden. But when he comes to eat and he is truly hungry, purple stripes show up on his sides. The stripes are like stripes on a marlin. Is it anger, or is it speed that brings out the stripes?

Chapter 17
The Dolphin

It was just before dark. The boat passed a great island of Sargasso weed. The weed heaved and swung in the light sea. It looked like the ocean was playing with friends under a yellow blanket.

A dolphin took the old man's small line. He saw it first when it jumped in the air. The dolphin was gold and he could see it in the last moments of sunlight. It was bending

and flapping in the air. It jumped again and again, tumbling in its fear. The man moved his way back to the boat and held the big line with his right hand and arm. He pulled the dolphin in with his left hand. He stepped on the line each time with his bare left foot.

When the fish was at the back of the boat, the fish jumped and twisted from side to side in desperation. The old man leaned over the boat and lifted up the shiny golden fish with its purple spots. Its jaws were biting the hook quickly. It hit the bottom of the boat with its long, flat body. He clubbed the fish across its shiny head, and then it shivered and stopped moving.

The old man unhooked the fish. He re-baited the line with another sardine and tossed it to the side of the boat. Then he went slowly back to the bow. He washed his left hand and wiped it on his trousers. He shifted the heavy line from his right hand to his left hand. He washed his right hand in the sea while he watched the sun set into the ocean and the direction of the fishing line.

"He hasn't changed at all," he said. But, as he watched the movement of the water against his hand, he noticed that it was clearly slower.

"I'll tie the two oars together across the back of the boat. This will slow down the fish in the night," he said. "He's good for the night, and so am I."

"It would be better to cut up the dolphin a little later to save the blood in the meat," he thought. "I can do that a little later, and then I could tie up the oars at the same time. I should keep the fish quiet now. I shouldn't disturb him too much at sunset. The setting of the sun is a difficult time for all fish."

He let his hand dry in the air, then he grasped the line with his right hand and eased himself as much as he could. He allowed himself to be pulled forward against the wood so that the boat took too more tension than he did.

"I'm learning how to do it," he thought. "In this situation, this is the way." He remembered the fish had not eaten since it took the bait. "And it is huge and needs a lot of food. I ate the whole bonito. Tomorrow I will eat the dolphin. He called the dolphin **dorado** in Spanish. Maybe I should eat some of it when I clean it. It will be harder to eat than the bonito. But nothing is easy.

"How do you feel, fish?" he asked out loud. "I feel good, and my left hand is better. I have food for a night and a day. Pull the boat, fish."

He did not truly feel good, because the pain from the line across his back had been there for so long. The pain changed into a dull feeling.

"But I have had worse things than that," he thought. "My

hand is only cut a little, and the cramp is gone from my left hand. My legs are doing better. Also, I am ahead of the fish now since I have eaten food."

It was dark now. It becomes dark quickly after the sun sets in September. He lay against the wood of the bow and rested as much as he could. The first stars came out. He did not know the name of the star was Rigel, but he saw it. He knew that soon they would all be out. He would see all his faraway friends.

"The fish is my friend too," he said out loud. "I have never seen or heard of such a fish. But I must kill him. I am glad we do not have to try to kill the stars."

"Imagine if a man had to kill the moon. The moon always runs away," he thought. "Imagine if a man had to try to kill the sun? We were born lucky."

Then he felt sorry for the great fish that had nothing to eat. He felt sorry for the fish, and he did not hesitate. He still wanted to kill the fish.

"How many people will it feed," he thought. "But are they worthy to eat the fish? No, of course not. There is no one worthy of eating this honorable fish."

"I do not understand these things," he thought. "But it is good that we do not have to try to kill the sun, or the moon, or the stars. It is enough to just live on the sea and kill fish."

"Now, I must think about the drag. It has its risks and its benefits," he thought. "If the fish makes an effort and drags the boat with the oars, I might lose a lot of line and lose the fish. The boat is light, and this is uncomfortable, but it is safe. The fish is able to go very fast, but it hasn't used that skill yet. No matter what happens, I must cut up the dolphin so he does not spoil, and eat some of him for energy."

"Now, I will rest an hour more until I feel that he is stable and steady. I will decide before I do the work to tie the oars," he thought. "In the meantime, I can see how he acts and if he shows any changes. The oars are a good trick, but now is the time to play for safety. He still has energy, and I saw that the hook was in the corner of his mouth. He has kept his mouth shut tight. The punishment of the hook is nothing. But the punishment of hunger and fighting against unknown forces is everything."

"Rest now, old man, and let him work until your next duty comes."

Chapter 18
Sleep

He rested for what he thought was two hours. The moon did not rise now until late in the night. He had no way of telling time. He wasn't resting either; he was just a little more relaxed than he was before. He was still bearing the pull of the fishing line across his shoulders. He placed his left hand on the wood of the bow. He put more and more of the fish's resistance onto the boat itself.

"It would be simple if I could tie up the line somewhere," he thought. "But with one small move, he could break the line. I must support the pull of the line with my body and be ready to let out the line with both hands."

"But you have not slept yet, old man," he said out loud. "It is half a day and a night and now another day, and you have not slept. You must devise a way so that you sleep a little while the fish is quiet. If you do not sleep, you might become unclear in the head."

"I'm clear enough in the head," he thought. "I am very clear. I am as clear as the stars that are my brothers."

"Still, I must sleep. The stars sleep. The moon and the sun go to sleep. Even the ocean goes to sleep when there is no current and it is calm. Remember to sleep," he thought. "Make yourself do it and think of a way to take care of the fishing lines."

"Now go back and prepare the dolphin. It is too dangerous to tie the oars as a drag if you need sleep."

"I could go without sleeping," he told himself. "But it would be too dangerous."

He started to work his way back to the stern on his hands and knees. He was careful and he tried not to surprise the fish.

"The fish may be half asleep himself," he thought. "But I do not want him to rest. He must pull until he dies."

In the back of the boat, he turned so that his left hand held the line tightly across his shoulders. He drew his knife from its sheath with his right hand. The stars were bright now, and he saw the dolphin. He pushed the blade of his knife into the dolphin's head and drew him out from under the back of the boat. He put one of his feet on the fish and split him quickly from the tail to the tip of his jaw. Then he put his knife down and gutted him with his right hand. He was scooping him clean and pulling the gills clear. He felt the throat, it was heavy and slippery in his hands. He slit it open. There were two flying fish inside. They were fresh and hard. He laid them side by side and dropped the guts and the gills over the back of the boat. They sank and left a trail of dim light in the water. The dolphin was cold and grayish white in the starlight. The old man skinned one side of him while he held his right foot on the fish's head. Then he turned him over and skinned the other side. He cut each side off the dolphin from the head down to the tail.

He pushed the dolphin's bones overboard. He looked to see if there was a ripple in the water. But there was only the dim light as it sank down. He turned around and placed the two flying fish inside the two pieces of the dolphin. He put his knife back in its sheath. He walked slowly back to the bow. His back was bent under the weight of the fishing line. He carried the fish in his right hand.

He laid the two pieces of fish out on the wood with the flying fish in the bow of the boat. After that, he put the line across his shoulders in a new place. He held the line again with his left hand resting on the boat. Then he leaned over the side of the boat and washed the flying fish in the water. He felt the speed of the water against his hand. His hand was metallic from skinning the fish and he watched the flow of the water against it. The flow of the water was less strong, and as he rubbed his hand against the boat, metallic particles from the fish floated off and drifted away slowly to the back side of the boat.

"He is tiring, or he is resting," the old man said. "Now, let me finish eating this dolphin and get some rest and a little sleep."

Under the stars and with the night growing colder, he ate half of one of the dolphin pieces and one of the flying fish.

"Dolphin is an excellent fish to eat when it's cooked," he said. "And what a terrible fish it is to eat raw. I will never go in a boat again without salt or limes."

"If I had a brain, I would have splashed water on the bow of the boat all day, and it would have dried and left salt there," he thought. "But I did not hook the dolphin until the sun had almost set. This was because I did not prepare well. But, I chewed it all up, and I did not vomit."

In the sky, clouds were moving towards the east. One after another, the stars he knew were going away. It looked like he was moving into a great canyon of clouds. The wind had stopped.

"There will be bad weather in three or four days," he said. "But not tonight and not tomorrow. Tighten the line and get some sleep, old man, while the fish is calm and steady."

He held the line tight in his right hand and then pushed his thigh against his right hand. He leaned all his weight against the wood on the bow of the boat. Then he moved the line a little lower on his shoulders and it tightly in his left hand.

"My right hand can hold it as long as it is reinforced", he thought. "If my hand relaxes during sleep, my left hand will wake me as the line goes out. It is hard on the right hand. But he is used to challenges. Even if I sleep for twenty minutes or a half an hour, it is good."

He lay forward on the line with all of his body, putting all his weight onto his right band, and he fell asleep.

Chapter 19
A Cut on the Hand

He did not dream of the lions, but he dreamed of a large school of porpoises. They stretched for eight or ten miles. It was their mating season. They would leap high into the air and return into the same hole they had made in the water.

Then he dreamed that he was in the village on his bed. There was a north wind. He was very cold. His right arm was numb because he had slept on it instead of his pillow.

After that, he began to dream of the long yellow beach. He saw the first of the lions come down onto the beach. It was dusk, The other lions came. He rested his chin on the wood of the bow where the ship anchored. He could feel the evening breeze. He waited to see if there would be more lions, and he was happy.

The moon had been up for a long time. The old man slept on, and the fish continued to pull the boat. The boat moved into the tunnel of clouds.

He woke up to the jolt of his right fist hitting his face and the line slipping through his hand. The line burned as it slipped out of his hand. He had no feeling in his left hand, but he tried to stop it with his right hand, and the line rushed out. Finally, he held the left line with his hand and he leaned back against it. But now the line burned his back and his left hand. His left hand was cut by the line, and it took all the pressure from the fish.

He looked back at the coils of line, and they were becoming loose. Just then, the fish jumped and made a huge wave in the ocean. Then the fish fell again. The fish came up and jumped again and again. The boat was going fast and the line was also going out fast. The old man was holding the line at the breaking point. He had been pulled down tight onto the front of the boat. His face was stuck in the slice of dolphin, and he could not move.

"This is what we waited for. So, let's take it," he thought. "Make him pay for the line. Make him pay for it."

He could not see the fish jumping, but he only heard the ocean's current and the heavy splash as the fish fell. The fishing line was cutting his hands, but he knew this would happen. He tried to keep the line moving across the scarred part of his hands that had been cut before. He tried to not let the line slip into the palm of his hand or cut his fingers.

"If the boy was here, he would wet the coils of line," he thought. "Yes. If the boy were here. If the boy were here."

The line kept going out, but it was going out slowly. The old man was making the fish work hard to pull out every extra inch of line.

He got up and pulled his head out of the slice of fish that his cheek had fallen on. He was on his knees, and then he rose slowly to his feet. He was transferring the line, but he was doing it slowly. He went back to the coils of line. He could not see the coils, but he could feel them with his feet. There was still plenty of line in the boat. The fish had to pull more coils of line through the water.

"Yes, that's it," he thought. "And now he has jumped more than a dozen times. The sacks on his back are full of air, and he can't go down into the deep water where I can't find him. He will start circling soon, and then I must fight with him and make him exhausted. I wonder what startled him so suddenly? Was it hunger that made him wild, or was he scared by something in the night? Maybe he suddenly felt fear. But he was such a calm, strong fish, and he wasn't afraid. This is strange.

"You better be strong and confident, old man," he said. "You're holding him again, but you can't get more line. Soon he has to circle."

The old man held the line with his left hand and his shoulders. He leaned down and gathered water in his right hand to clean the dolphin particles off of his face. He was afraid that he would feel sick and vomit. He was scared that he would lose his strength.

When his face was cleaned off, he washed his right hand in the water over the side of the boat. He let his right hand stay in the saltwater while he watched the first light come out before the sunrise.

"He's headed almost east," he thought. "That means he is tired and going with the current. Soon he will have to circle back. Then our true work begins."

After his right hand had been in the water for a while, he took it out and looked at it.

"It is not bad," he said. "And pain does not matter to a man."

He held the line carefully. He did not want it to go into the fresh cuts in his hands. He switched hands and put his left hand into the sea on the other side of the boat.

"You did not do so badly for nothing," he said to his left hand. "But there was a moment when I could not find you."

"Why was I not born with two good hands?" he thought. "Maybe it was my fault that I didn't train both of my hands well. But, for goodness' sake, he has had enough chances to learn. Even though he had a cramp one time, he did a good job in the night. If he gets a cramp again, I will let the line cut him off."

He knew he was not thinking straight. He thought he should chew the piece of dolphin.

"But I can't," he told himself. "It is better to not think straight than to lose your strength from vomiting. And that dolphin piece was on my face. How can I eat it again? I will keep it for an emergency until it spoils. But it is too late to try to get stronger by eating more."

"You're stupid," he told himself. "Eat the other flying fish."

The flying fish was there. It was cleaned out and ready to eat. He picked it up with his left hand. He ate it, chewing the bones carefully and eating all of it.

"It has more nutrients than almost any other fish," he thought. "At least I can get the strength that I need. Now I have done what I can do. Let him begin to circle back and I will fight him."

Chapter 20
Circle

The fish started to swim in a circle. The sun was rising for the third time since the old man had gone out on the ocean to go fishing.

He could not tell by the direction of the line if the fish was swimming in a circle or not. It was too early for that. He felt the line lose some pressure. He began to pull on it gently with his right hand. It tightened, but just when he reached the point where it would break, the line began to come in.

He pulled out his shoulders and head from under the line. He began to pull in the line steadily and gently. He used both of his hands in a swinging motion. He tried to pull as much as he could with his body and legs. His old legs and shoulders rotated with the swinging of the pulling.

"It is a very big circle," he said. "But he is swimming in a circle." Then the line would not come in any more. He held it until he saw the drops of water jumping out from it. Then the line started going out. The old man knelt down and hesitated. Then he let the line go back into the water.

"He is swimming on the outside of his circle now," he said.

"I must hold on for as long as I can," he thought. "If I hold on tightly, his circle will get shorter each time. Maybe in an hour, I will get to see him. Now I must trick him. Then I can kill him."

But the fish kept swimming in a circle slowly. Two hours later, the old man was wet with sweat and his bones were tired. But the fish was making shorter circles. He could tell that the fish had risen up in the water.

For an hour, the old man had seen black spots in front of him. The sweat made his eyes feel salty. The sweat had salted the cut over his eye and on his forehead. He was not afraid of the black spots. He expected to see black spots, since he felt pressure in his body while he pulled on the line. However, he felt dizzy two times and felt like he was about to faint. That made him worried.

"I don't want to fail. I don't want to die while trying to fight this incredible fish," he said. "Now that the fish is finally coming closer, God, please help me to continue."I'll pray for one hundred Our Fathers and one hundred Ave Marias.

But I cannot say them now."

"I will gladly do this for you," he thought. "But I can't pray them now. I will have to pray them later."

Just then, he felt a sharp pulling on the line that he was holding. He felt a heavy feeling.

"He is hitting the wire leader with his spear," he thought. "I knew that was going to happen. This might make him jump, and I hope he just swims in circles now. If the fish jumps again, the hole where the hook is will open up and he can escape from the hook."

"Don't jump, fish," he said. "Don't jump."

The fish hit the wire several times more. Each time the fish shook his head, and the old man gave him a little more line.

"I must keep him where he is while he is in pain," he thought. My pain does not matter. I can control my pain. But his pain could make him go mad."

After a while, the fish stopped hitting at the wire and started swimming slowly in a circle again. The old man was pulling the fish closer. But he felt faint again. He lifted up some sea water with his left hand and put it on his head. Then he splashed more on his head and rubbed the back of his neck.

"I have no cramps," he said. "He'll swim up soon and I can survive. You have to survive. Don't even mention it."

He kneeled against the bow. He slipped the line over his back again for just a moment.

"I'll rest now while he makes a circle, then I will stand up and fight him when he comes in," he decided.

He was tempted to rest in the bow. He wanted to let the fish make a circle on his own without pulling the line for him. But the line was tight and the fish turned around and was coming toward the boat. The old man rose to his feet and started rotating and pulling in the line again.

"I'm more tired than I have ever been," he thought.

Now the wind from the east is getting stronger. But that will help me bring the fish back home. I really need help with that.

"I'll rest when the fish swims around again," he said. "I feel much better now. In two or three more circles, I will catch this fish.

His straw hat was on the back of his head. He sat down in the bow as he felt the fish make a circle in the water.

"You do the work, fish," he thought. "I'll meet you when you turn around."

The sea was rising. But there was a calm breeze and good weather, and the old man needed the breeze to get home.

"I will sail the boat southwest," he said. "A man is never really lost at sea. This is a long island."

Chapter 21
The Death of the Marlin

He first saw the fish on its third time swimming around the boat. He saw the fish first as a dark shadow that took a long time to pass under the boat. The old man could not believe how long the fish was.

"No," he said. "He can't be that big."

But the fish really was that big. He came to the surface only thirty yards away when he finished swimming in a circle. The man saw his tail come out of the water. It was higher than a big machete blade and a very light lavender color above the dark blue water. The fish's tail swept back and as the fish swam just below the surface of the water, the old man could see his huge size. He had purple stripes on his body. His back fin was down and his pectoral fins were spread out.

This time, when the fish swam in a circle, the old man could see the fish's eye. There were two gray sucker fish that swam around the fish. Sometimes they were attached to him. Sometimes they swam away from the fish. Sometimes they would swim in his shadow. Both of the sucker fish were over three feet long. When they swam fast, they twisted their bodies like eels.

The old man was sweating now but his sweat was from something other than the sun. Every time the fish turned calmly in the water, the old man was pulling in more line. After the fish turned two more times, the old man was sure that he would have a chance to pierce the fish with the harpoon.

"But I must let him come close, close, close," he thought. "I should not try to pierce the head. I should pierce the heart."

"Be calm and strong, old man," he said.

The fish's back was out of the water the next time he swam in a circle, but he was a little too far from the boat. He was still too far away on the next circle, but he was higher out of the water. The old man was sure that if he pulled in more fishing line, he could pull the fish next to the boat. He had prepared his harpoon a long time ago. He also had a coil of light rope ready in a round basket. The rope fastened tightly to the bow of the boat.

The fish returned from making his circle. The fish was calm and beautiful, and only his great tail was moving. The old man pulled as hard as he could to bring him closer. For just a moment, the fish turned a little on his side. Then he straightened himself and began another circle.

"I moved him," the old man said. "I moved him just then."

He felt like he was going to faint again, but he held on to the great fish with all his strength.

"I moved him," he thought. "Maybe this time I can pull him over the side."

"Pull, hands pull," he thought. "Hang in there, legs. Hold on, head. Hold on for me. You never let me down. This time, I'll pull the fish over the side."

But when the old man worked with all his effort and pulled with all his strength, the fish pulled back and then swam ahead.

"Fish," the old man said. "Fish, you are going to have to die anyway. Do you have to kill me too?"

"Nothing will happen then," he thought.

His mouth was too dry to speak, but he could not reach for the water.

"I must get him to come along the side of the boat this time," he thought.

"I am not able to handle more turns. Yes, you are," he told himself. "You will stay strong forever."

On the next turn, he nearly had the fish. But the fish straightened himself and swam slowly away again.

"You are killing me, fish," the old man thought. "But you have a right to do that. I have never seen a greater, or a calmer, or a more beautiful fish than you, brother. Come on and kill me. I do not care who kills who."

"Now you are getting confused in the head," he thought. "You must clear your head. Suffer like a man."

"Clear up, head," he said in a voice he couldn't really hear. "Clear up."

The fish did the same thing two more times as it turned around.

"I do not know," the old man thought.

He felt like he was going to faint each time.

"I do not know. But I will try again once more."

He tried to catch it again and he felt like fainting. The fish straightened out and swam away slowly with its tail waving in the air.

"I'll try again," the old man promised.

His hands were weak and he could not see well. He tried again, and the same thing happened. He spent some time thinking, and he felt faint before he tried again. "I will try once more."

The old man took all his pain, strength, and pride, and he used them to fight the fish. The fish came closer to the boat and swam gently on his side. His beak almost touched the boat. The fish started to pass by the boat. It was long, wide, and silver with purple stripes.

The old man dropped the line and he put his foot on it. He lifted the harpoon as high as he could and he drove it down with all his strength. He thrust it into the side of the fish just behind its fin. The man felt the harpoon go in and he leaned on it and pushed it down with all his weight.

Then the fish moved for the last time. The fish came up and showed his great length, width, power, and beauty. He seemed to hang in the air above the old man. Then he fell into the water with a big splash. Water sprayed all over the old man and the boat.

The old man felt faint and sick. He could not see well. He cleared the harpoon line and let it slip slowly through his hands. He saw the fish was on his back with his silver belly up. The harpoon was sticking out of the fish. The sea was dyed red with the blood from his heart. At first it was as dark as a school of fish in the blue water. Then it spread like a cloud. The fish was silvery and floated on the waves.

Chapter 22
Tying the Marlin to the Boat

The old man looked ahead carefully for a short moment. He led the harpoon line around the bow of the boat two times. He hid his head in his hands.

"I must keep my head up and stay strong," he said as he leaned against the wood of the bow. "I am a tired old man. But I have killed this fish, who is my brother. Now I must do the hard work."

"Now I must prepare the rope to fasten him to the side of the boat," he thought. "Even if there were two of us here and we flooded the boat to put the fish inside, the boat could not hold him. I must prepare everything and pull the fish closer. Then I will fasten him well, raise up the mast, and sail home.

He started to pull the fish to the side of the boat so that he could thread a line through the gills of the fish and tie his head to the bow.

"I want to see him and to touch and to feel him. He is my treasure," he thought. "But that is not why I wish to feel him."

"When I pushed the harpoon into him, I think I felt his heart," he thought. "I will bring him in now and tie him tightly to the side of the boat."

"Get to work, old man," he said. He took a little drink of water. "There's a lot of hard work to be done now that the fight is over."

He looked up at the sky and then looked out to his fish. He looked at the sun carefully.

"It's probably a few minutes past noon," he thought. "And the wind from the east is rising. The lines all mean nothing now. The boy and I will tie them again when I get home."

"Come on, fish," he said.

But the fish did not come. The fish lay there, floating in the sea. The old man pulled the boat up to him.

He had the fish's head against the bow. Even when he was with the fish, he could not believe its size. He untied the harpoon rope from the bow and threaded it through the fish's gills and out through his jaws. He looped the rope around his sword and threaded it through the fish's other gill. He fastened it to the bow. He cut the rope and then went to the back of the boat to tie the tail. The fish had turned silver from his original shades of purple and silver. The stripes were the same color as his tail and they were wider than a man's hand with his fingers spread out. The fish's eye looked as disconnected as the mirrors in a periscope.

"That was the only way to kill him," the old man said. He felt better after drinking the water. He knew he would not lose his mind, and his head was clear.

"The fish is over fifteen hundred pounds," he thought. "Maybe much more. If the head, tail, and fins are removed, two-thirds of that will be thirty cents a pound. Is that right?"

"I need a pencil for that," he said. "My head is not that clear. But I think the great DiMaggio would be proud of me today. I did not have any bone spurs. But my hands and my back really hurt."

"I wonder what a bone spur is," he thought. "Maybe we have them without realizing it."

He tied the fish to the bow, the stern, and the middle of the boat. The fish was so big, it was like tying another big boat beside his boat. The old man cut a piece of line. He tied the fish's lower jaw against the top of his pointed mouth. He did this so that the fish's mouth would not open, and they could sail as smoothly as possible. Then he raised the mast. He had his spear and the pole of his sail was in place. The patched sail opened up and the boat began to move. The boat began to move. The man was half lying in the back of the boat as he sailed southwest.

He did not need a compass to tell him where southwest was. He only needed to feel the wind and the movement of the sail. "I should put out a small line with bait on it. I could try to catch something to eat and drink the water inside." But he could not find the bait. His sardines had spoiled. So he hooked a piece of yellow Gulf weed with his gaff. He shook the yellow Gulf weed and the small shrimps that were in it fell onto the planking of the boat. There were more than a dozen of them. They jumped and kicked like fleas in the sand. The old man removed their heads with his thumb and index finger. He ate them and he chewed up the shells and the tails. They were very tiny, but he knew they were nourishing. They tasted good.

The old man still had two drinks of water left in the bottle. He drank half of one after he had eaten the shrimps. The boat was sailing well, even with the difficulties. The old man steered with the lever under his arm. He could see the fish. He could see his hands and feel his back against the wood of the boat. He knew that this really did happen. It was not a dream. There was a moment, when he was feeling terrible, he thought perhaps it was a dream. Then when the fish had come up out of the water and hung there without moving, he thought that something was not right. He could not believe it. At that time, he was not able to see very well. Now, he was able to see just fine.

Now he knew the fish was real. The pain in his hands and his back was not a dream.

"The hands will cure quickly," he thought. The bleeding stopped, and the salt water will heal them. The dark water of the gulf is the greatest healer. All I have to do is keep my head clear. My hands have done their work, and we sail well together. The fish's mouth is closed and his tail is set straight. We are sailing like brothers.

Then his head started to become a little unclear. "Is the

fish bringing me in, or am I bringing the fish in? If I pulled him from behind, or if the fish was in the boat, this would not be a question. But we are sailing together, side by side."

"If it makes the fish happy, he can bring me in. I'm only better than the fish because I tricked him. He didn't hurt me." The old man thought to himself.

Chapter 23
The Mako Shark

They sailed well, and the old man soaked his hands in the salt water. He tried to keep his head clear. There were high clouds above them and the old man knew the breeze would last all night. The old man looked at the fish continuously to make sure it was true. It was an hour before the first shark arrived.

The shark was not a surprise. The shark had come up from deep down in the water. The dark cloud of blood had dissolved in the deep sea. The shark had come up so fast and without warning. He broke through the surface of the blue water and was out in the sun. Then he fell back into the sea and sniffed the smell and started tracking down the course of the boat.

Sometimes the shark lost track of the scent, but he would pick up the scent again. He continued on the course and swam very fast. He was a very big Mako shark, and he was able to swim as fast as the fastest fish in the sea. Everything about this shark was beautiful, except his jaws. His back was like a swordfish's back, and his belly was silver. His skin was smooth and good-looking. His body was like a swordfish, except for his huge jaws, which were shut. He swam quickly under the surface of the water. The high fin on his back cut through the water without shaking. On the inside of his jaws, there were eight rows of teeth. All of the teeth were pointing inwards. They were not shaped like the teeth of normal sharks. They were shaped like a man's fingers when they were grasping something. The teeth were almost as long as the fingers of the old man. They had razor-sharp cutting edges on both sides. Sharks are built to feed on all the fish in the sea. Sharks are fast, strong, and well-armed. They have no other enemies. Now the shark speeded up as he smelled the newer scent. His blue-black fin cut through the water.

When the old man saw him coming, he knew that the shark had no fear at all. The shark would do what he wanted. The old man prepared the harpoon and fastened the rope to it while he watched the shark come up. The rope was short because he had cut some of it away to tie up the fish.

The old man's head was clear now. He was determined, but he didn't have much hope. This was a good moment, but it will be over soon, he thought. He looked at the great fish as he watched the shark come close.

"I wish this was all just a dream," he thought. I cannot keep the shark from hitting me, but maybe I can kill him.

"Mako shark," he thought. "I don't like you! I wish you bad luck!"

The shark came close to the back of the boat. When the shark hit the fish, the old man saw his mouth open and his strange eyes. He heard the sound of the shark's teeth biting into the body of the fish. The shark bit into the fish above its tail. The shark's head was out of the water and his back was coming out too. The old man could hear the noise of the skin ripping on the big fish. He shoved the harpoon down into the shark's head between his eyes and nose. He saw the shark's sharp, blue head and its big eyes and jaws. He hit it right where the brain was. He hit it with his aching hands. He shoved the harpoon with all his strength. He hit the shark without hope, but with determination and a desire to kill it.

The shark swayed in the water, and the old man saw his eye was not alive. Then he turned over once again, wrapping himself with the rope. The old man knew that he was dead, but the shark would not accept it. Then, the shark's tail started beating the water and his jaws were clicking. The shark splashed over the water as a speedboat does. The water was white where his tail had slapped it. Three-quarters of his body was clear above the water. The rope became tight and it shook. Then the rope broke. The old man watched the shark. He lay peacefully for a little while on the surface of the water. Then he went down very slowly.

"He took about forty pounds of meat from the fish," the old man said out loud.

"He took my harpoon too and all the rope," he thought. "Now my fish is bleeding again, and there will be other sharks."

He did not like to look at the fish anymore since he had been wounded. When the fish had been hit, the old man felt like he had been hit too.

"But I killed the shark that hit my fish," he thought. "And he was the biggest Mako shark that I have ever seen. And, God knows, I have seen big sharks.

"This moment was too good to last," he thought. "I wish it had been a dream now and that I had never hooked the fish. I wish I was alone in bed reading the newspapers."

"But man is not made for defeat," he said. "A man can be destroyed, but not defeated."

"I am sorry that I killed the fish though," he thought. "Now, the bad time is coming, and I do not even have the harpoon. The Mako sharks are cruel and able and strong and intelligent. But I was more intelligent than he was."

"Perhaps not," he thought. "Perhaps I was only better because I had a harpoon."

"Don't think, old man," he said out loud. "Sail on this course and face the moment when it comes."

"But I must think," he thought. "Because it is all I have left—that and baseball. I wonder how the great DiMaggio would have liked the way I hit the shark in the brain?"

"It wasn't that difficult," he thought. "Any man could do it. But I wonder if the wounds on my hands were as much of a challenge as having bone spurs. I cannot know. I never had anything wrong with my heel, except that time when I stepped on a ray and it stung me."

"Think about something cheerful, old man," he said. "Every minute, you are closer to home. You are sailing freely because your boat lost forty pounds."

He knew the pattern of what could happen when he reached the current. But there was nothing he could do.

"Yes there is," he said out loud. "I can tie my knife to one of the oars."

So he tied his knife to an oar. While he did that, the lever was under his arm and the sail was under his foot.

"Now," he said. "I am still an old man. But I am not unarmed."

The breeze was fresh now, and he sailed on well. He only watched the front part of the fish. Some of his hope returned.

"It is silly not to hope," he thought. Besides, I believe it is a sin not to hope."

"Do not think about sin," he thought. "There are enough problems now without sin. Also, I have no understanding of sin. I am not sure if I believe in sin. Perhaps it was a sin to kill the fish. But I killed it to keep myself alive and feed many people. If you think like that, anything could be a sin."

"Do not think about sin," he said to himself. "You were born to be a fisherman just like the fish was born to be a fish. Saint Peter was a fisherman too."

But he liked to think about everything that he was involved in. There was nothing to read and he did not have a radio. So he thought a lot, and he kept on thinking about sin.

"You did not kill the fish only to keep it alive and to sell it for food," he thought. "You killed the fish because of your pride and because you are a fisherman. You loved him when he was alive, and you loved him after he died. If you love him, it is not a sin to kill him. Or is it more of a sin?"

"You think too much, old man," he said out loud.

"But you enjoyed killing the Mako shark," he thought.

"He catches the fish alive, just like you do. He does not eat dead fish. He is not hungry for anything, like other sharks. He is beautiful and great and he is not afraid of anything.

"I killed him in self-defense," the old man said out loud. "And I killed him well."

"Besides," he thought, "Everything kills everything else in some way. Fishing kills me and it also keeps me alive."

"No, it's the boy who keeps me alive," he thought. "I have to be honest with myself."

He leaned over the side of the boat. He pulled a piece of the meat from the fish where the shark had cut him. He chewed it and felt its quality and its good taste. It was firm and juicy, like meat, but it was not red. He knew that it would bring the highest price In the market. But there was no way to keep the fish's smell out of the water. The old man knew that a very hard time was coming.

Chapter 24
The Two Sharks

The breeze was steady. It had blown further into the north-east. He knew that meant that it would not stop. The old man looked ahead of him, but he could not see sails. He could not see boats or the smoke of any ships. Only flying fish flew from one side of his boat to the other side and yellow Gulf sea weed floated in the sea. He could not even see a bird.

He had sailed for two hours, resting in the boat. Sometimes he chewed a bit of the meat from the marlin. He was trying to rest and to be strong.

Suddenly he saw the first of two sharks, "Ay," he said out loud.

There is no translation for this word. Perhaps it is like the noise a man would make if a nail went through his hands.

"Shark," he said out loud.

He had seen the second fin now coming up behind the first. He knew that they were shovel-nosed sharks by their brown, triangular fins and the dull movements of their tails. They found the scent and they were excited. They were very hungry. They were so excited that they were losing the scent and then finding it again. But they were closing in more and more.

The old man fastened the sail and the lever. Then he

picked up the oar with the knife tied to it. He lifted it as lightly as he could because his hands were in pain. Then he opened and closed his hands on it softly. He closed his hands tightly so they would take the pain. He watched the sharks coming. He could see their wide, flat, shovel-pointed heads now and their wide pectoral fins. These sharks were full of hate and they smelled bad. They ate living things and dead things. When they were hungry, they would bite at an oar or part of a boat. These sharks would cut the legs of turtles when they were sleeping on the surface of the water. They would bite a man in the water if they were hungry, even if the man did not smell like fish blood.

"Ay," the old man said. "Sharks. Come on, Sharks."

They came. But they did not come as the Mako had come. One shark turned and went out of sight under the boat. The old man could feel the boat shake as he bit and pulled on the fish. The other shark watched the old man with his yellow eyes. Then he swam up fast with his half circle of jaws to bite the fish. The middle of the shark's head showed clearly between the top of his brown head and back. The old man shoved his knife into the middle of the shark's head. He shoved the knife again into the shark's cat-like, yellow eyes. The shark let go of the fish and slid down into the water, swallowing what he had taken as he died.

The boat was still shaking because of the other shark. The shark was destroying the fish. The old man untied the sail line so that the boat would swing to the side and the shark would come out. When he saw the shark, he leaned over the side and punched with his knife. He only hit the shark's muscle, and the skin was so thick, he could hardly get the knife in. The attack hurt the man's hands and shoulders. But the shark came up fast with his head out and he bit the fish. The old man hit him in the center of his flat head. The old man removed the knife and punched the shark in the exact same spot again. He hung on to the fish with his jaws. The old man hit him in his left eye. The shark still hung there.

"No?" the old man said, and he shoved the knife to the middle of the shark's head. It was an easy shot now, and he felt the bone split. The old man turned the oar around and put the flat blade between the shark's jaws to open them. He twisted the oar. The shark slid into the water.

"Go on, Shark. Slide down a mile deep. Go see your friend," he said.

The old man wiped the blade of his knife and put down the oar. Then he found the sail line, and the sail filled with wind. He brought the boat onto her course.

Chapter 25
The Broken Knife

"They must have taken a quarter of him," he said out loud. "I wish it were a dream and that I had never hooked him. I'm sorry about it, fish. This makes
everything feels wrong."
He stopped to say all of this. He did not want to look at the fish now. The fish's blood drained out and his color was gone. He was a silver color now, like the back of a mirror.

"I shouldn't have gone out so far. It was too far for you and for me, fish. I'm sorry, fish."
"Now," he said to himself. "Look at the rope tied to the knife and see if it has been cut. Then get your hands ready, because there is still more to do."

"I wish I had a stone for the knife," the old man said after he checked it. "I should have brought a stone."
"You should have brought many things," he thought. "But you did not bring them, old man. Now is no time to think about what you do not have. Think about what you can do with what you have."
"You give me a lot of good advice," he said out loud. "But I'm tired of it."

He held the lever under his arm. He dipped both his hands in the water as the boat sailed forward.

"I have no idea how much of the fish that shark took," he said. "But the boat is much lighter now."

He did not want to think of the bottom part of the fish, which was destroyed. He knew with each bite the shark had taken, meat had been torn away. The fish now mad a trail for all the sharks to smell, like a highway through the sea.

"This fish would have kept me busy all winter," he thought. "Don't think of that. Just rest and prepare your hands to protect the fish."

The blood smell from my hands means nothing now with the blood smell making a trail in the water. Besides, my hands do not bleed much. There are no deep cuts. The bleeding may keep my left hand from cramping.

"What can I think of now?" he thought. "Nothing. I must think of nothing and wait for the next ones."

"I wish it had been a dream," he thought. "But who knows? The dream might have turned out well."

The next shark that came was a shovel-nosed shark. He came up like a hungry pig coming to its food. The shark's mouth was so big, a person could fit their head in it. The old man let him chew on the fish, and then he shoved the knife on the oar down into his brain. The shark pulled back as he rolled. The knife blade snapped.

The old man went back and started to sail. He did not even watch the big shark sinking slowly into the water. First the shark was life-size, then small, then very tiny as it sank into the water. In the past, that always made the old man excited. But the old man did not even watch it now.

"I have the gaff now," he said. "But it will do no good. I have the two oars, the lever, and the short club."

"Now the sharks have beaten me," he thought. "I am too old to club sharks to death. But I will try it for as long as I can. " I have the oars, the short club, and the lever."

He dipped his hands in the water again. It was getting late in the afternoon. He saw nothing but the sea and the sky. There was more wind in the sky than there was before. He hoped that he would see land.

"You're tired, old man," he said. "You're tired inside."

Sharks did not come to the boat again until just before sunset. The old man saw their brown fins coming along the wide way the fish make in the water. They were not even thinking about the smell of the blood. They were headed straight for the boat, swimming side by side.

He pushed the lever to stop the boat. He fastened the sail line and reached under the stem for the club. It was made from a broken oar. It was about two and a half feet in length. He could only use the club with one hand. He held the club in his right hand and watched the sharks come. They were both shovel-nosed sharks.

"I must let the first shark get the fish and then I have to hit him on the point of the nose or straight across the top of the head," he thought.

The two sharks closed in on the boat together. When he saw the shark nearest to him open his jaws, it took a bite out of the silver part of the fish. The old man raised the club high and brought it down. The club slammed on to the top of the shark's head. He felt the rubbery solid surface of the shark's head as the club came down. He felt the hardness of bone too. He hit the shark once more across the point of the nose. The shark slid down from the fish.

The other shark had gone in and out and came in again. His jaws were wide open. The old man could see pieces of the fish in the corner of his mouth. The shark chewed on the fish and closed his jaws. The old man swung at him and hit only the head. The shark looked at him and pulled away another piece of the fish. The old man slammed the club down on him again as he moved away. As he hit the shark, it felt like solid rubber.

"Come on, shark," the old man said. "Come in again."
The shark came in a rush. The old man hit him as he closed his mouth. He lifted the club as high up as he could and shoved it down. This time he felt the bone at the bottom of the shark's head. The old man hit the shark again while the shark chewed up the meat slowly and slid down from the fish.

The old man watched for the shark to come again, but neither shark came. Then he saw one shark on the surface swimming in circles. He did not see the fin of the other shark.

"I could not expect to kill them," he thought. "In that moment I could have killed them. I did hurt them both badly, though. They probably don't feel very good. "If I had a bat and used two hands, I could have killed the first one. I could have killed it now," he thought.

Chapter 26
Half of the Fish

He did not want to look at the fish. He knew that the sharks destroyed half of the fish. The sun went down while he was fighting the sharks.

"It will be dark soon," he said. "Then I should see the lights of Havana. If I am too far to the East, I will see the lights of one of the new beaches."

"I cannot be too far out now," he thought. "I hope no one has been too worried. The boy is the only one who would worry, of course. But I know he trusts in me."

"Many of the older fishermen will worry. Many others will worry too," he thought. "I live in a good town."

He could not talk to the fish anymore. The fish had been ruined too badly. Then something came into his head.

"Half fish," he said. "Fish that you were. I am sorry that I went too far out. I ruined you and me. But we have killed many sharks. We ruined many others. How many did you ever kill, old fish? You do not have that spear on your head for nothing."

He liked to think of the fish and what he could do to a shark.

"I should have cut the spear off of the fish's nose to fight them," he thought. "But I don't have an ax, and I don't have a knife. But if I had the fish's spear, I could tie it to an oar. That would be the best weapon. We could have fought them together."

"What will you do now if they come in the night? What can you do?"

"Fight them," he said. "I'll fight them until I die."

He was in the dark with no glow and no lights. There

was only the wind and the movement of the sail. He felt that perhaps he was already dead. He put his two hands together and felt his palms. They were not dead. He could feel that he was alive by feeling the pain of opening and closing them. He leaned back against the boat. He knew he was not dead. His shoulders told him.

"I have all those prayers I promised to pray if I caught the fish," he thought. "But I am too tired to say them now. I had better get the sack and put it over my shoulders."

He lay in the boat and sailed and watched for the light to come in the sky.

"I have half of the fish," he thought. "Maybe I'll have the luck to bring part of the fish home. I should have some luck."

"No," he said. "You wasted your luck when you went too far outside."

"Don't be silly," he said out loud. "And keep awake and sail. You may have some luck yet."

"I'd like to buy some if there's any place they sell it," he said.

"What could I buy luck with?" he asked himself. "Could I buy it with a lost harpoon and a broken knife and two injured hands?"

"You might," he said. "You tried to buy it with eighty-four days at sea. They nearly sold it to you too."

"I must not think nonsense," he thought. "Luck is a thing that comes in many forms. Who can recognize luck?

I would take some luck in any form and pay what they asked for it."

"I wish I could see the glow from the lights," he thought. "I am wishing for too many things. But that is the thing I want for now."

He tried to settle more comfortably to sail the boat. He felt more pain and he knew he was not dead.

Chapter 27
The Last Fight

He saw the reflection of the city's lights. It must have been around ten o'clock at night. The lights looked like the dim light in the sky before the moon rose. The lights were dim, but they were bright enough to be seen from across the ocean. The breeze was getting stronger. He thought that he would reach the edge of the stream soon.

"Now it is over," he thought. "The sharks will probably come at me again. But what can a man do to fight against them in the dark without a weapon?"

He was stiff and sore now, and his wounds and his tired body were hurting. It was so cold that night.

"I hope I do not have to fight again," he thought. "I hope so much that I do not have to fight again."

But by midnight, he fought more sharks, and this time he knew the fight was useless. They came in a pack. He could see the lines that the shark's fins made in the water. He saw the glow of the shark's skin as they jumped on the fish to eat it. He hit their heads with his club and he felt them under the boat. He hit them wildly. He couldn't see them, but he could feel them and hear them. He felt something grab his club, and then it was gone.

He pulled the lever from the boat and beat the sharks with it. He held the lever in both hands and shoved it down again and again. The sharks went up to the front of the boat together and tore off pieces of the fish. The sharks turned around and came back again for more.

Finally, a shark came to the fish's head. The old man knew that the fight was over. He swung the lever across the shark's head where the shark held the fish's head in his jaws. He swung again and again. He heard the lever break, and he pushed at the shark with the broken part. He felt the shark go down into the shark. He knew the lever was sharp, so he shoved it into the shark again. The shark let go and rolled away. That was the last shark of the pack that came. There was nothing more for them to eat.

The old man could hardly breathe. He had a strange taste in his mouth. It was coppery and sweet, and he was afraid of it for a moment. But there was not much of it.

He spat into the ocean and said, "Eat that, sharks. And imagine that you've killed a man."

He knew the sharks beat him completely. He went back to the stern and found the lever. He pushed the lever into the slot of the rudder so he could sail the boat. He placed the sack around his shoulders and put the boat on its course.

He sailed lightly now. He had no thoughts or feelings at all. He was past everything now. He sailed the boat to make it back to his home port as well as he could. In the night, sharks chewed on the fish's bones. The sharks chewed on the fish like a person might pick up pieces of food under a table. The old man did not pay attention to them. He only paid attention to sailing. The only other thing he noticed was how well the boat sailed. The weight of the fish was gone from the side of the boat.

"She's good," he thought. "She is safe and not harmed in any way except for the lever. That is easy to fix."

He felt that he was inside the current. He could see the lights of the beach along the shore. He knew where he was now, and it was not hard to get home.

"The wind is our friend, anyway," he thought.

Then he added, "Sometimes the wind is our friend. Sometimes the great sea is our friend, and it's full of friends and enemies."

"And my bed," he thought. "My bed is my friend. Just my bed. To go to bed will be a great thing. It is easy when you are beaten. I never knew how easy it was."

"And what beat you?" he thought.

"Nothing," he said out loud. "I went out too far."

When he sailed into the little harbor, the Terrace's lights were out. He knew everyone was in bed. The breeze had risen and was blowing strongly now. But it was quiet in the harbor. He sailed up onto a place below the rocks. There was no one to help him, so he pulled the boat up as far as he could. He stepped out and tied the boat to a rock.

He pulled on the mast and rolled up the sail and tied it. Then he shouldered the mast and started to climb. He began to feel how tired he really was. He stopped for a moment and looked back. He saw the tail of the fish sticking out from behind the boat. He saw the white line of the fish's backbone and the dark shape of the fish's head. He saw the long sharp nose of the fish and everything in between.

He started to climb again. He came to the top and fell down. He lay there for a while with the mast across his shoulder. He tried to get up, but it was too difficult. He sat there with the mast on his shoulder and he looked at the road. A cat passed by and the old man watched it. Then he just watched the road.

Finally, he put the mast down and stood up. He picked the mast up and put it on his shoulder, and started up the road. He had to sit down five times before he reached his hut. Inside the hut, he leaned the mast against the wall. In the dark, he found a water bottle and took a drink. Then he lay down on the bed. He pulled the blanket over his shoulders, then over his back and legs. He slept with his face down on the newspapers. His arms were out straight and the palms of his hands were up.

Chapter 28
At Home

He was asleep when the boy looked in the door in the morning. The wind was blowing so hard that some boats would not be going out. The boy had slept in late and then come to the old man's hut to check if he was there. The boy had come every morning to check. The boy saw that the old man was breathing. Then he saw the old man's hands. He started to cry. He went out very quietly to go to bring him some coffee. He was crying while he went down the road.

Many fishermen were around the boat. They were looking at the fish's bones tied beside it. One of the fishermen was in the water. He rolled up his pants. He measured the skeleton with a line. The boy did not go down. He had been there before, and one of the fishermen was taking care of the boat for the boy.

"How is he?" one of the fishermen shouted. "Sleeping," the boy called. The boy did not care that they saw him crying.

"Don't let anyone bother him."

"He was eighteen feet from nose to tail," the fisherman who was measuring the fish called.

"I believe it," the boy said.

He went into the Terrace and asked for a can of coffee.

"I want the coffee hot and with plenty of milk and sugar in it."

"Anything more?"

"No. Afterwards, I will see what he can eat."

"What a fish it was," the proprietor said. "There has never been a fish like this one. You caught two fish yesterday too."

"Never mind my fish," the boy said, and he started to cry again.

"Would you like a drink of any kind?" the proprietor asked.

"No," the boy said. "Tell them not to bother Santiago. I'll be back."

"Tell Santiago how sorry I am."

"Thanks," the boy said.

The boy carried the hot can of coffee up to the old man's hut and sat by him until he woke up. At one time, it looked like he was waking up. But then he went back into a deep sleep. The boy went out to borrow some wood to heat the coffee. Finally the old man woke up.

"Don't sit up," the boy said. "Drink this."

He poured some of the coffee into a glass. The old man took it and drank it.

"They beat me, Manolin," he said. "They truly beat me."

"He didn't beat you. Not the fish."

"No. Truly. That happened after I caught the fish."

"Pedrico is looking after the boat and the gear. What do you want to be done with the fish's head?"

"Let Pedrico chop it up to use in fish traps."

"And the spear?"

"You keep it if you want it."

"I want it," the boy said. "Now, we must make our plans about other things."

"Did they search for me?"

"Of course. They searched for you with the coast guard and with planes."

"The ocean is very big, and a boat is small and hard to see," the old man said.

He noticed how nice it was to have someone to talk to instead of talking to himself.

"I missed you," he said. "What did you catch?"

"I caught one on the first day, one on the second day, and two on the third day," the boy said.

"Very good."

"Now we will fish together again."

"No. I am not lucky. I am not lucky anymore."

"Don't tell me about luck," the boy said. "I'll bring the luck with me."

"What will your family say?"

"I don't care. I caught fish yesterday. I still have much to learn from you. We will fish together now."

"We must get a good killing spear and always have it on the boat with us. You can make the blade from part of an old Ford car. We can make it when we go to Guanabacoa together. It should be sharp, so it won't break. My knife broke."

"I'll get a knife and start to make a spear from the car parts."

"Do we have any windy days ahead?"

"We might have three windy days. Maybe more."

"I will have everything ready," the boy said. "Let your hands recover, old man."

"I know how to care for my hands. I spat something strange in the night. It felt like something in my chest was broken."

"Take care of that too," the boy said. "Lie down, old man, and I will bring you your clean shirt. I will bring you something to eat."

"Bring any of the newspapers from the time that I was gone," the old man said.

"You must get better quickly. There is so much I need to learn from you. You can teach me everything. Did you suffer a lot?"

"I did suffer a lot," the old man said.

"I'll bring the food and the newspapers," the boy said. "Rest well, old man. I will bring something from the pharmacy for your hands."

"Don't forget to tell Pedrico that the fish's head is his."

"I will remember."

As the boy went out the door and down the coral rock road, he was crying again. That afternoon, there was a party at the Terrace. Many rich people were taking a tour.

They looked down at the empty beer cans and dead fish by the sea. One woman saw the fishing boat and the long, white bones of the fish. She saw the huge tail that lifted and swung in the water while the wind blew.

"What's that?" she asked a waiter. She pointed to the bones of the great fish.

"Tiburon," the waiter said. "It's a shark." He wanted to try and explain what had happened.

"I didn't know sharks had such handsome, beautiful tails."

"I didn't either," her boyfriend said.

Up the road, in his hut, the old man was sleeping again. He was still sleeping on his face. The boy was sitting by him. The boy was watching him. The old man was dreaming about the lions.

이제 다 왔습니다.
당신은 벌써 노인과 바다를 4번 읽었습니다.
자신 있게, 노인과 바다를 원문을 읽어 보세요.
읽다가 모르는 단어가 나오면 다시 Level 4로 내려가서
해당 문단을 읽어보세요.

LEVEL 5

"Be patient, hand," he said. "I do this for you." I wish I could feed the fish, he thought. He is my brother. But I must kill him and keep strong to do it. Slowly and conscientiously he ate all of the wedge-shaped strips of fish. He straightened up, wiping his hand on his trousers.

Chapter 1
The Old Man and the Boy

He was an old man who fished alone in a skiff in the Gulf Stream, and he had gone eighty-four days now without taking a fish. In the first forty days, a boy had been with him. But after forty days without a fish, the boy's parents had told him that the old man was now definitely and finally '***salao***', which is the worst form of unlucky, and the boy had gone at their orders in another boat which caught three good fish the first week.

It made the boy sad to see the old man come in each day with his skiff empty, and he always went down to help him carry either the coiled lines or the gaff and harpoon and the sail that was furled around the mast.

The sail was patched with flour sacks and, furled, it looked

like the flag of permanent defeat.

The old man was thin and gaunt with deep wrinkles in the back of his neck. The brown blotches of the benevolent skin cancer the sun brings from its reflection on the tropic sea were on his cheeks. The blotches ran well down the sides of his face, and his hands had the deep-creased scars from handling heavy fish on the cords. But none of these scars were fresh. They were as old as erosions in a fishless desert.

Everything about him was old except his eyes, and they were the same color as the sea and were cheerful and undefeated.

"Santiago," the boy said to him as they climbed the bank from where the skiff was hauled up. "I could go with you again. We've made some money."

The old man had taught the boy to fish, and the boy loved him.

"No," the old man said. "You're with a lucky boat. Stay with them."

"But remember how you went eighty-seven days without fish, and then we caught big ones every day for three weeks."

"I remember," the old man said. "I know you did not leave me because you doubted."

"It was papa made me leave. I am a boy, and I must obey him."

"I know," the old man said. "It is quite normal."

"He hasn't much faith."

"No," the old man said. "But we have. Haven't we?"

"Yes," the boy said. "Can I offer you a beer on the Terrace, and then we'll take the stuff home."

"Why not?" the old man said. "Between fishermen."

They sat on the Terrace, and many of the fishermen made fun of the old man, and he was not angry. Others, of the older fishermen, looked at him and were sad. But they did not show it, and they spoke politely about the current and the depths they had drifted their lines at and the steady good weather and of what they had seen.

Chapter 2
Friendship

The successful fishermen of that day were already in and had butchered their marlin out and carried them laid full length across two planks, with two men staggering at the end of each plank, to the fish house where they waited for the ice truck to carry them to the market in Havana.

Those who had caught sharks had taken them to the shark factory on the other side of the cove where they were hoisted on a block and tackle, their livers removed, their fins cut off and their hides skinned out and their flesh cut into strips for salting.

When the wind was in the east a smell came across the harbor from the shark factory, but today there was only the faint edge of the odor because the wind had backed into the north and then dropped off and it was pleasant and sunny on the Terrace.

"Santiago," the boy said.

"Yes," the old man said. He was holding his glass and thinking of many years ago.

"Can I go out to get sardines for you for tomorrow?"

"No. Go and play baseball. I can still row and Rogelio will throw the net."

"I would like to go. If I cannot fish with you. I would like to serve in some way."

"You bought me a beer," the old man said. "You are already a man."

"How old was I when you first took me in a boat?"

"Five and you nearly were killed when I brought the fish in too green and he nearly tore the boat to pieces. Can you remember?"

"I can remember the tail slapping and banging and the thwart breaking and the noise of the clubbing. I can remember you throwing me into the bow where the wet coiled lines were and feeling the whole boat shiver and the noise of you clubbing him like chopping a tree down and the sweet blood smell all over me."

"Can you really remember that or did I just tell it to you?"

"I remember everything from when we first went together."

The old man looked at him with his sun-burned, confident, loving eyes.

"If you were my boy I'd take you out and gamble," he said. "But you are your father's and your mother's and you are in a lucky boat."

"May I get the sardines? I know where I can get four baits too."

"I have mine left from today. I put them in salt in the box."

"Let me get four fresh ones."

"One," the old man said. His hope and his confidence had never gone. But now they were freshening as when the breeze rises.

"Two," the boy said.

"Two," the old man agreed. "You didn't steal them?"

"I would," the boy said. "But I bought these."

"Thank you," the old man said. He was too simple to wonder when he had attained humility. But he knew he had attained it and he knew it was not disgraceful and it carried no loss of true pride.

"Tomorrow is going to be a good day with this current," he said.

"Where are you going?" the boy asked.

"Far out to come in when the wind shifts. I want to be out before it is light."

"I'll try to get him to work far out," the boy said. "Then if you hook something truly big we can come to your aid."

"He does not like to work too far out."

"No," the boy said. "But I will see something that he cannot see such as a bird working and get him to come out after dolphin."

"Are his eyes that bad?"

"He is almost blind."

"It is strange," the old man said. "He never went turtle-ing. That is what kills the eyes."

"But you went turtle-ing for years off the Mosquito Coast and your eyes are good."

"I am a strange old man"

"But are you strong enough now for a truly big fish?"

"I think so. And there are many tricks."

"Let us take the stuff home," the boy said. "So I can get the cast net and go after the sardines."

They picked up the gear from the boat. The old man carried the mast on his shoulder and the boy carried the wooden box with the coiled, hard-braided brown lines, the gaff, and the harpoon with its shaft. The box with the baits was under the stern of the skiff along with the club that was used to subdue the big fish when they were brought alongside. No one would steal from the old man but it was better to take the sail and the heavy lines home as the dew was bad for them and, though he was quite sure no local people would steal from him, the old man thought that a gaff and a harpoon were needless temptations to leave in a boat.

Chapter 3
The Shack

They walked up the road together to the old man's shack and went in through its open door. The old man leaned the mast with its wrapped sail against the wall and the boy put the box and the other gear beside it. The mast was nearly as long as the one room of the shack.

The shack was made of the tough budshields of the royal palm which are called *guano* and in it there was a bed, a table, one chair, and a place on the dirt floor to cook with charcoal. On the brown walls of the flattened, overlapping leaves of the sturdy fibered *guano* there was a picture in color of the Sacred Heart of Jesus and another of the Virgin of Cobre. These were relics of his wife. Once there had been a tinted photograph of his wife on the wall but he had taken it down because it made him too lonely to see it and it was on the shelf in the corner under his clean shirt.

"What do you have to eat?" the boy asked.

"A pot of yellow rice with fish. Do you want some?"

"No. I will eat at home. Do you want me to make the fire?"

"No. I will make it later on. Or I may eat the rice cold."

"May I take the cast net?"

"Of course."

There was no cast net and the boy remembered when they had sold it. But they went through this fiction every day. There was no pot of yellow rice and fish and the boy knew this too.

"Eighty-five is a lucky number," the old man said. "How would you like to see me bring one in that dressed out over a thousand pounds?"

"I'll get the cast net and go for sardines. Will you sit in the sun in the doorway?"

"Yes. I have yesterday's paper and I will read the baseball."

The boy did not know whether yesterday's paper was a fiction too. But the old man brought it out from under the bed.

"Perico gave it to me at the bodega," he explained. "I'll be back when I have the sardines. I'll keep yours and mine together on ice and we can share them in the morning. When I come back you can tell me about the baseball."

"The Yankees cannot lose."

"But I fear the Indians of Cleveland."

"Have faith in the Yankees my son. Think of the great DiMaggio."

"I fear both the Tigers of Detroit and the Indians of Cleveland."

"Be careful or you will fear even the Reds of Cincinnati and the White Sox of Chicago."

"You study it and tell me when I come back."

"Do you think we should buy a terminal of the lottery with an eighty-five? Tomorrow is the eighty-fifth day."

"We can do that," the boy said. "But what about the eighty-seven of your great record?"

"It could not happen twice. Do you think you can find an eighty-five?"

"I can order one."

"One sheet. That's two dollars and a half. Who can we borrow that from?"

"That's easy. I can always borrow two dollars and a half."

"I think perhaps I can too. But I try not to borrow. First you borrow. Then you beg."

"Keep warm old man," the boy said. "Remember we are in September."

"The month when the great fish come," the old man said. "Anyone can be a fisherman in May."

"I go now for the sardines," the boy said.

When the boy came back the old man was asleep in the chair and the sun was down. The boy took the old army blanket off the bed and spread it over the back of the chair and over the old man's shoulders. They were strange shoulders, still powerful although very old, and the neck was still strong too and the creases did not show so much when the old man was asleep and his head fallen forward. His shirt had been patched so many times that it was like the sail and the patches were faded to many different shades by the sun. The old man's head was very old though and with his eyes closed there was no life in his face. The newspaper lay across his knees and the weight of his arm held it there in the evening breeze. He was barefooted.

Chapter 4
The Baseball game

The boy left him there and when he came back the old man was still asleep.

"Wake up old man," the boy said and put his hand on one of the old man's knees.

The old man opened his eyes and for a moment he was coming back from a long way away. Then he smiled.

"What have you got?" he asked.

"Supper," said the boy. "We're going to have supper."

"I'm not very hungry."

"Come on and eat. You can't fish and not eat."

"I have," the old man said getting up and taking the newspaper and folding it. Then he started to fold the blanket.

"Keep the blanket around you," the boy said. "You'll not fish without eating while I'm alive."

"Then live a long time and take care of yourself," the old man said. "What are we eating?"

"Black beans and rice, fried bananas, and some stew."

The boy had brought them in a two-decker metal container from the Terrace. The two sets of knives and forks and spoons were in his pocket with a paper napkin wrapped around each set.

"Who gave this to you?"

"Martin. The owner."

"I must thank him."

"I thanked him already," the boy said. "You don't need to thank him."

"I'll give him the belly meat of a big fish," the old man said. "Has he done this for us more than once?"

"I think so."

"I must give him something more than the belly meat then. He is very thoughtful for us."

"He sent two beers."

"I like the beer in cans best."

"I know. But this is in bottles, Hatuey beer, and I take back the bottles."

"That's very kind of you," the old man said.

"Should we eat?"

"I've been asking you to," the boy told him gently. "I have not wished to open the container until you were ready."

"I'm ready now," the old man said. "I only needed time to wash."

Where did you wash? the boy thought. The village water supply was two streets down the road. I must have water here for him, the boy thought, and soap and a good towel. Why am I so thoughtless? I must get him another shirt and a jacket for the winter and some sort of shoes and another blanket.

"Your stew is excellent," the old man said.

"Tell me about the baseball," the boy asked him.

"In the American League it is the Yankees as I said," the old man said happily.

"They lost today," the boy told him.

"That means nothing. The great DiMaggio is himself again."

"They have other men on the team."

"Naturally. But he makes the difference. In the other league, between Brooklyn and Philadelphia I must take Brooklyn. But then I think of Dick Sisler and those great drives in the old park."

"There was nothing ever like them. He hits the longest ball I have ever seen."

"Do you remember when he used to come to the Terrace?"

"I wanted to take him fishing but I was too timid to ask him. Then I asked you to ask him and you were too timid."

"I know. It was a great mistake. He might have gone with

us. Then we would have that for all of our lives."

"I would like to take the great DiMaggio fishing," the old man said. "They say his father was a fisherman. Maybe he was as poor as we are and would understand."

"The great Sisler's father was never poor and he, the father, was playing in the Big Leagues when he was my age."

"When I was your age I was before the mast on a square rigged ship that ran to Africa and I have seen lions on the beaches in the evening."

"I know. You told me."

"Should we talk about Africa or about baseball?"

"Baseball I think," the boy said. "Tell me about the great John J. McGraw." He said Jota for J.

"He used to come to the Terrace sometimes too in the older days. But he was rough and harsh-spoken and difficult when he was drinking. His mind was on horses as well as baseball. At least he carried lists of horses at all times in his pocket and frequently spoke the names of horses on the telephone."

"He was a great manager," the boy said. "My father thinks he was the greatest."

"Because he came here the most times," the old man said. "If Durocher had continued to come here each year your father would think him the greatest manager."

"Who is the greatest manager, really, Luque or Mike Gonzalez?"

"I think they are equal."

"And the best fisherman is you."

"No. I know others better."

"**Que Va**," the boy said. "There are many good fishermen and some great ones. But there is only you."

"Thank you. You make me happy. I hope no fish will come along so great that he will prove us wrong."

"There is no such fish if you are still strong as you say."

"I may not be as strong as I think," the old man said. "But I know many tricks and I have resolution."

"You ought to go to bed now so that you will be fresh in the morning. I will take the things back to the Terrace."

"Good night then. I will wake you in the morning."

"You're my alarm clock," the boy said.

"Age is my alarm clock," the old man said.

"Why do old men wake so early? Is it to have one longer day?"

"I don't know," the boy said. "All I know is that young boys sleep late and hard."

"I can remember it," the old man said. "I'll waken you in time."

"I do not like for him to waken me. It is as though I were inferior."

"I know."

"Sleep well old man."

Chapter 5
Going Fishing

The boy went out. They had eaten with no light on the table and the old man took off his trousers and went to bed in the dark. He rolled his trousers up to make a pillow, putting the newspaper inside them. He rolled himself in the blanket and slept on the other old newspapers that covered the springs of the bed.

He was asleep in a short time and he dreamed of Africa when he was a boy and the long golden beaches and the white beaches, so white they hurt your eyes, and the high capes and the great brown mountains. He lived along that coast now every night and in his dreams he heard the surf roar and saw the native boats come riding through it. He smelled the tar and oakum of the deck as he slept and he smelled the smell of Africa that the land breeze brought at morning.

Usually when he smelled the land breeze he woke up and dressed to go and wake the boy. But tonight the smell of the land breeze came very early and he knew it was too early in his dream and went on dreaming to see the white peaks of the Islands rising from the sea and then he dreamed of the different harbours and roadsteads of the Canary Islands.

He no longer dreamed of storms, nor of women, nor of great occurrences, nor of great fish, nor fights, nor contests of strength, nor of his wife. He only dreamed of places now and of the lions on the beach. They played like young cats in the dusk and he loved them as he loved the boy. He never dreamed about the boy. He simply woke, looked out the open door at the moon and unrolled his trousers and put them on. He urinated outside the shack and then went up the road to wake the boy. He was shivering with the morning cold. But he knew he would shiver himself warm and that soon he would be rowing.

The door of the house where the boy lived was unlocked and he opened it and walked in quietly with his bare feet. The boy was asleep on a cot in the first room and the old man could see him clearly with the light that came in from the dying moon. He took hold of one foot gently and held it until the boy woke and turned and looked at him. The old man nodded and the boy took his trousers from the chair by the bed and, sitting on the bed, pulled them on.

The old man went out the door and the boy came after him. He was sleepy and the old man put his arm across his shoulders and said, "I am sorry."

"*Qua Va*," the boy said. "It is what a man must do."

They walked down the road to the old man's shack and all along the road, in the dark, barefoot men were moving, carrying the masts of their boats.

When they reached the old man's shack the boy took

the rolls of line in the basket and the harpoon and gaff and the old man carried the mast with the furled sail on his shoulder.

"Do you want coffee?" the boy asked.

"We'll put the gear in the boat and then get some."

They had coffee from condensed milk cans at an early morning place that served fishermen.

"How did you sleep old man?" the boy asked. He was waking up now although it was still hard for him to leave his sleep.

"Very well, Manolin," the old man said. "I feel confident today."

"So do I," the boy said. "Now I must get your sardines and mine and your fresh baits. He brings our gear himself. He never wants anyone to carry anything."

"We're different," the old man said. "I let you carry things when you were five years old."

"I know it," the boy said. "I'll be right back. Have another coffee. We have credit here."

He walked off, bare-footed on the coral rocks, to the ice house where the baits were stored. The old man drank his coffee slowly. It was all he would have all day and he knew that he should take it. For a long time now eating had bored him and he never carried a lunch. He had a bottle of water in the bow of the skiff and that was all he needed for the day.

The boy was back now with the sardines and the two baits wrapped in a newspaper and they went down the trail to the skiff, feeling the pebbled sand under their feet, and lifted the skiff and slid her into the water.

"Good luck old man."

"Good luck," the old man said. He fitted the rope lashings of the oars onto the thole pins and, leaning forward against the thrust of the blades in the water, he began to row out of the harbour in the dark. There were other boats from the other beaches going out to sea and the old man heard the dip and push of their oars even though he could not see them now the moon was below the hills.

Chapter 6
Bait

Sometimes someone would speak in a boat. But most of the boats were silent except for the dip of the oars. They spread apart after they were out of the mouth of the harbour and each one headed for the part of the ocean where he hoped to find fish. The old man knew he was going far out and he left the smell of the land behind and rowed out into the clean early morning smell of the ocean.

He saw the phosphorescence of the Gulf weed in the water as he rowed over the part of the ocean that the fishermen called the great well because there was a sudden deep of seven hundred fathoms where all sorts of fish congregated because of the swirl the current made against the steep walls of the floor of the ocean. Here there were concentrations of shrimp and bait fish and sometimes schools of squid in the deepest holes and these rose close to the surface at night where all the wandering fish fed on them.

In the dark the old man could feel the morning coming and as he rowed he heard the trembling sound as flying fish left the water and the hissing that their stiff set wings made as they soared away in the darkness. He was very fond of flying fish as they were his principal friends on the ocean.

He was sorry for the birds, especially the small delicate dark terns that were always flying and looking and almost never finding, and he thought, the birds have a harder life than we do except for the robber birds and the heavy strong ones. Why did they make birds so delicate and fine as those sea swallows when the ocean can be so cruel? She is kind and very beautiful. But she can be so cruel and it comes so suddenly and such birds that fly, dipping and hunting, with their small sad voices are made too delicately for the sea.

He always thought of the sea as **la mar** which is what people call her in Spanish when they love her. Sometimes those who love her say bad things of her but they are always said as though she were a woman. Some of the younger fishermen, those who used buoys as floats for their lines and had motorboats, bought when the shark livers had brought much money, spoke of her as el mar which is masculine. They spoke of her as a contestant or a place or even an enemy. But the old man always thought of her as feminine and as something that gave or withheld great favours, and if she did wild or wicked things it was because she could not help them. The moon affects her as it does a woman, he thought.

He was rowing steadily and it was no effort for him since he kept well within his speed and the surface of the ocean was flat except for the occasional swirls of the current. He was letting the current do a third of the work and as it started to be light he saw he was already further out than he had hoped to be at this hour. I worked the deep wells for a week and did nothing, he thought. Today I'll work out where the schools of bonito and albacore are and maybe there will be a big one with them.

Before it was really light he had his baits out and was drifting with the current. One bait was down forty fathoms. The second was at seventy-five and the third and fourth were down in the blue water at one hundred and one hundred and twenty-five fathoms. Each bait hung head down with the shank of the hook inside the bait fish, tied and sewed solid and all the projecting part of the hook, the curve and the point, was covered with fresh sardines.

Each sardine was hooked through both eyes so that they made a half-garland on the projecting steel. There was no part of the hook that a great fish could feel which was not sweet smelling and good tasting.

The boy had given him two fresh small tunas, or albacores, which hung on the two deepest lines like plummets and, on the others, he had a big blue runner and a yellow jack that had been used before; but they were in good condition still and had the excellent sardines to give them scent and attractiveness. Each line, as thick around as a big pencil, was looped onto a green-sapped stick so that any pull or touch on the bait would make the stick dip and each line had two forty-fathom coils which could be made fast to the other spare coils so that, if it were necessary, a fish could take out over three hundred fathoms of line.

Now the man watched the dip of the three sticks over the side of the skiff and rowed gently to keep the lines straight up and down and at their proper depths. It was quite light and any moment now the sun would rise.The sun rose thinly from the sea and the old man could see the other boats, low on the water and well in toward the shore, spread out across the current. Then the sun was brighter and the glare came on the water and then, as it rose clear, the flat sea sent it back at his eyes so that it hurt sharply and he rowed without looking into it.

He looked down into the water and watched the lines

that went straight down into the dark of the water. He kept them straighter than anyone did, so that at each level in the darkness of the stream there would be a bait waiting exactly where he wished it to be for any fish that swam there. Others let them drift with the current and sometimes they were at sixty fathoms when the fishermen thought they were at a hundred. But, he thought, I keep them with precision. Only I have no luck any more. But who knows? Maybe today. Every day is a new day. It is better to be lucky. But I would rather be exact. Then when luck comes you are ready.

Chapter 7
A Man-Of-War Bird

The sun was two hours higher now and it did not hurt his eyes so much to look into the east. There were only three boats in sight now and they showed very low and far inshore. All my life the early sun has hurt my eyes, he thought. Yet they are still good. In the evening I can look straight into it without getting the blackness. It has more force in the evening too. But in the morning it is painful.

Just then he saw a man-of-war bird with his long black wings circling in the sky ahead of him. He made a quick drop, slanting down on his back-swept wings, and then circled again.

"He's got something," the old man said aloud. "He's not just looking."

He rowed slowly and steadily toward where the bird was circling. He did not hurry and he kept his lines straight up and down. But he crowded the current a little so that he was still fishing correctly though faster than he would have fished if he was not trying to use the bird.

The bird went higher in the air and circled again, his wings motionless. Then he dove suddenly and the old man saw flying fish spurt out of the water and sail desperately over the surface.

"Dolphin," the old man said aloud. "Big dolphin."

He shipped his oars and brought a small line from under the bow. It had a wire leader and a medium-sized hook and he baited it with one of the sardines. He let it go over the side and then made it fast to a ring bolt in the stern. Then he baited another line and left it coiled in the shade of the bow. He went back to rowing and to watching the long-winged black bird who was working, now, low over the water.

As he watched the bird dipped again slanting his wings for the dive and then swinging them wildly and ineffectually as he followed the flying fish. The old man could see the slight bulge in the water that the big dolphin raised as they followed the escaping fish. The dolphin were cutting through the water below the flight of the fish and would be in the water, driving at speed, when the fish dropped. It is a big school of dolphin, he thought. They are widespread and the flying fish have little chance. The bird has no chance. The flying fish are too big for him and they go too fast.

He watched the flying fish burst out again and again and the ineffectual movements of the bird. That school has gotten away from me, he thought. They are moving out too fast and too far. But perhaps I will pick up a stray and perhaps my big fish is around them. My big fish must be somewhere.

The clouds over the land now rose like mountains and the coast was only a long green line with the gray blue hills behind it. The water was a dark blue now, so dark that it was almost purple. As he looked down into it he saw the red sifting of the plankton in the dark water and the strange light the sun made now. He watched his lines to see them go straight down out of sight into the water and he was happy to see so much plankton because it meant fish.

The strange light the sun made in the water, now that the sun was higher, meant good weather and so did the shape of the clouds over the land. But the bird was almost out of sight now and nothing showed on the surface of the water but some patches of yellow, sun-bleached Sargasso weed and the purple, formalized, iridescent, gelatinous bladder of a Portuguese man-of-war floating dose beside the boat. It turned on its side and then righted itself. It floated cheerfully as a bubble with its long deadly purple filaments trailing a yard behind it in the water.

"*Agua mala*," the man said. "You whore."

From where he swung lightly against his oars he looked down into the water and saw the tiny fish that were coloured like the trailing filaments and swam between them and under the small shade the bubble made as it drifted. They were immune to its poison. But men were not and when some of the filaments would catch on a line and rest there slimy and purple while the old man was working a fish, he would have welts and sores on his arms and hands of the sort that poison ivy or poison oak can give. But these poisonings from the *agua mala* came quickly and struck like a whiplash.

The iridescent bubbles were beautiful. But they were the falsest thing in the sea and the old man loved to see the big sea turtles eating them. The turtles saw them, approached them from the front, then shut their eyes so they were completely carapaced and ate them filaments and all. The old man loved to see the turtles eat them and he loved to walk on them on the beach after a storm and hear them pop when he stepped on them with the horny soles of his feet.

He loved green turtles and hawk-bills with their elegance and speed and their great value and he had a friendly contempt for the huge, stupid loggerheads, yellow in their armour-plating, strange in their love-making, and happily eating the Portuguese men-of-war with their eyes shut.

He had no mysticism about turtles although he had gone in turtle boats for many years. He was sorry for them all, even the great trunk backs that were as long as the skiff and weighed a ton. Most people are heartless about turtles because a turtle's heart will beat for hours after he has been cut up and butchered. But the old man thought, I have such a heart too and my feet and hands are like theirs. He ate the white eggs to give himself strength. He ate them all through May to be strong in September and October for the truly big fish.

He also drank a cup of shark liver oil each day from the big drum in the shack where many of the fishermen kept their gear. It was there for all fishermen who wanted it. Most fishermen hated the taste. But it was no worse than getting up at the hours that they rose and it was very good against all colds and grippes and it was good for the eyes.

Chapter 8
Albacore

Now the old man looked up and saw that the bird was circling again.

"He's found fish," he said aloud. No flying fish broke the surface and there was no scattering of bait fish. But as the old man watched, a small tuna rose in the air, turned and dropped head first into the water. The tuna shone silver in the sun and after he had dropped back into the water another and another rose and they were jumping in all directions, churning the water and leaping in long jumps after the bait. They were circling it and driving it.

If they don't travel too fast I will get into them, the old man thought, and he watched the school working the water white and the bird now dropping and dipping into the bait fish that were forced to the surface in their panic.

"The bird is a great help," the old man said. Just then the stern line came taut under his foot, where he had kept a loop of the line, and he dropped his oars and felt the tile weight of the small tuna's shivering pull as he held the line firm and commenced to haul it in. The shivering increased as he pulled in and he could see the blue back of the fish in the water and the gold of his sides before he swung him over the side and into the boat. He lay in the stern in the sun, compact and bullet shaped, his big, unintelligent eyes staring as he thumped his life out against the planking of the boat with the quick shivering strokes of his neat, fast-moving tail. The old man hit him on the head for kindness and kicked him, his body still shuddering, under the shade of the stern.

"Albacore," he said aloud. "He'll make a beautiful bait. He'll weigh ten pounds."

He did not remember when he had first started to talk aloud when he was by himself. He had sung when he was by himself in the old days and he had sung at night sometimes when he was alone steering on his watch in the smacks or in the turtle boats.

He had probably started to talk aloud, when alone, when the boy had left. But he did not remember. When he and the boy fished together they usually spoke only when it was necessary. They talked at night or when they were storm-bound by bad weather. It was considered a virtue not to talk unnecessarily at sea and the old man had always considered it so and respected it. But now he said his thoughts aloud many times since there was no one that they could annoy.

"If the others heard me talking out loud they would think that I am crazy," he said aloud. "But since I am not crazy, I do not care. And the rich have radios to talk to them in their boats and to bring them the baseball."

Now is no time to think of baseball, he thought. Now is the

time to think of only one thing. That which I was born for. There might be a big one around that school, he thought. I picked up only a straggler from the albacore that were feeding. But they are working far out and fast. Everything that shows on the surface today travels very fast and to the north-east. Can that be the time of day? Or is it some sign of weather that I do not know?

He could not see the green of the shore now but only the tops of the blue hills that showed white as though they were snow-capped and the clouds that looked like high snow mountains above them. The sea was very dark and the light made prisms in the water. The myriad flecks of the plankton were annulled now by the high sun 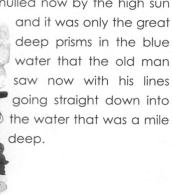 and it was only the great deep prisms in the blue water that the old man saw now with his lines going straight down into the water that was a mile deep.

Chapter 9
Encounter

The tuna, the fishermen called all the fish of that species tuna and only distinguished among them by their proper names when they came to sell them or to trade them for baits, were down again. The sun was hot now and the old man felt it on the back of his neck and felt the sweat trickle down his back as he rowed. I could just drift, he thought, and sleep and put a bight of line around my toe to wake me. But today is eighty-five days and I should fish the day well.

Just then, watching his lines, he saw one of the projecting green sticks dip sharply.

"Yes," he said. "Yes," and shipped his oars without bumping the boat. He reached out for the line and held it softly between the thumb and forefinger of his right hand. He felt no strain nor weight and he held the line lightly. Then it came again. This time it was a tentative pull, not solid nor heavy, and he knew exactly what it was. One hundred fathoms down a marlin was eating the sardines that covered the point and the shank of the hook where the hand-forged hook projected from the head of the small tuna.

The old man held the line delicately, and softly, with his left hand, unleashed it from the stick. Now he could let it run through his fingers without the fish feeling any tension. This far out, he must be huge in this month, he thought. Eat them, fish. Eat them. Please eat them. How fresh they are and you down there six hundred feet in that cold water in the dark. Make another turn in the dark and come back and eat them. He felt the light delicate pulling and then a harder pull when a sardine's head must have been more difficult to break from the hook. Then there was nothing.

"Come on," the old man said aloud. "Make another turn. Just smell them. Aren't they lovely? Eat them good now and then there is the tuna. Hard and cold and lovely. Don't be shy, fish. Eat them."

He waited with the line between his thumb and his finger, watching it and the other lines at the same time for the fish might have swum up or down. Then came the same delicate pulling touch again.

"He'll take it," the old man said aloud. "God help him to take it."

He did not take it though. He was gone and the old man felt nothing.

"He can't have gone," he said. "Christ knows he can't have gone. He's making a turn. Maybe he has been hooked before and he remembers something of it."

Then he felt the gentle touch on the line and he was happy.

"It was only his turn," he said. "He'll take it."

He was happy feeling the gentle pulling and then he felt something hard and unbelievably heavy. It was the weight of the fish and he let the line slip down, down, down, unrolling off the first of the two reserve coils. As it went down, slipping lightly through the old man's fingers, he still could feel the great weight, though the pressure of his thumb and finger were almost imperceptible.

"What a fish," he said. "He has it sideways in his mouth now and he is moving off with it."

Then he will turn and swallow it, he thought. He did not say that because he knew that if you said a good thing it might not happen. He knew what a huge fish this was and he thought of him moving away in the darkness with the tuna held crosswise in his mouth. At that moment he felt him stop moving but the weight was still there. Then the weight increased and he gave more line. He tightened the pressure of his thumb and finger for a moment and the weight increased and was going straight down.

"He's taken it," he said. "Now I'll let him eat it well."

He let the line slip through his fingers while he reached down with his left hand and made fast the free end of the two reserve coils to the loop of the two reserve coils of the next line. Now he was ready. He had three forty-fathom coils of line in reserve now, as well as the coil he was using.

"Eat it a little more," he said. "Eat it well."

Eat it so that the point of the hook goes into your heart

and kills you, he thought. Come up easy and let me put the harpoon into you. All right. Are you ready? Have you been long enough at table?

"Now!" he said aloud and struck hard with both hands, gained a yard of line and then struck again and again, swinging with each arm alternately on the cord with all the strength of his arms and the pivoted weight of his body.

Nothing happened. The fish just moved away slowly and the old man could not raise him an inch. His line was strong and made for heavy fish and he held it against his back until it was so taut that beads of water were jumping from it. Then it began to make a slow hissing sound in the water and he still held it, bracing himself against the thwart and leaning back against the pull. The boat began to move slowly off toward the north-west.

The fish moved steadily and they travelled slowly on the calm water. The other baits were still in the water but there was nothing to be done.

"I wish I had the boy" the old man said aloud. "I'm being towed by a fish and I'm the towing bitt. I could make the line fast. But then he could break it. I must hold him all I can and give him line when he must have it. Thank God he is travelling and not going down."

What I will do if he decides to go down, I don't know. What I'll do if he sounds and dies I don't know. But I'll do something. There are plenty of things I can do.

He held the line against his back and watched its slant in the water and the skiff moving steadily to the north-west. This will kill him, the old man thought. He can't do this forever. But four hours later the fish was still swimming steadily out to sea, towing the skiff, and the old man was still braced solidly with the line across his back.

"It was noon when I hooked him," he said. "And I have never seen him."

He had pushed his straw hat hard down on his head before he hooked the fish and it was cutting his forehead. He was thirsty too and he got down on his knees and, being careful not to jerk on the line, moved as far into the bow as he could get and reached the water bottle with one hand. He opened it and drank a little. Then he rested against the bow. He rested sitting on the un-stepped mast and sail and tried not to think but only to endure.

Then he looked behind him and saw that no land was visible. That makes no difference, he thought. I can always come in on the glow from Havana. There are two more hours before the sun sets and maybe he will come up before that. If he doesn't, maybe he will come up with the moon. If he does not do that maybe he will come up with the sunrise. I have no cramps and I feel strong. It is he that has the hook in his mouth. But what a fish to pull like that. He must have his mouth shut tight on the wire. I wish I could see him. I wish I could see him only once to know what I have against me.

Chapter 10
Moving Along

The fish never changed his course nor his direction all that night as far as the man could tell from watching the stars. It was cold after the sun went down and the old man's sweat dried cold on his back and his arms and his old legs. During the day he had taken the sack that covered the bait box and spread it in the sun to dry. After the sun went down he tied it around his neck so that it hung down over his back and he cautiously worked it down under the line that was across his shoulders now. The sack cushioned the line and he had found a way of leaning forward against the bow so that he was almost comfortable. The position actually was only somewhat less intolerable; but he thought of it as almost comfortable.

I can do nothing with him and he can do nothing with me, he thought. Not as long as he keeps this up.

Once he stood up and urinated over the side of the skiff and looked at the stars and checked his course. The line showed like a phosphorescent streak in the water straight out from his shoulders. They were moving more slowly now and the glow of Havana was not so strong, so that he knew the current must be carrying them to the eastward. If I lose the glare of Havana we must be going more to the eastward, he thought. For if the fish's course held true

I must see it for many more hours.

I wonder how the baseball came out in the grand leagues today, he thought. It would be wonderful to do this with a radio. Then he thought, think of it always. Think of what you are doing. You must do nothing stupid.

Then he said aloud, "I wish I had the boy. To help me and to see this."

No one should be alone in their old age, he thought. But it is unavoidable. I must remember to eat the tuna before he spoils in order to keep strong. Remember, no matter how little you want to, that you must eat him in the morning. Remember, he said to himself.

During the night two porpoises came around the boat and he could hear them rolling and blowing. He could tell the difference between the blowing noise the male made and the sighing blow of the female.

"They are good," he said. "They play and make jokes and love one another. They are our brothers like the flying fish."

Then he began to pity the great fish that he had hooked. He is wonderful and strange and who knows how old he is, he thought. Never have I had such a strong fish nor one who acted so strangely. Perhaps he is too wise to jump. He could ruin me by jumping or by a wild rush. But perhaps he has been hooked many times before and he knows that this is how he should make his fight. He cannot know that it is only one man against him, nor that it is an old man. But what a great fish he is and what will he bring in the market if the flesh is good. He took the bait like a male and he pulls like a male and his fight has no panic in it. I wonder if he has any plans or if he is just as desperate as I am?

He remembered the time he had hooked one of a pair of marlin. The male fish always let the female fish feed first and the hooked fish, the female, made a wild, panic-stricken, despairing fight that soon exhausted her, and all the time the male had stayed with her, crossing the line and circling with her on the surface. He had stayed so close that the old man was afraid he would cut the line with his tail which was sharp as a scythe and almost of that size and shape.

When the old man had gaffed her and clubbed her, holding the rapier bill with its sandpaper edge and dubbing her across the top of her head until her colour turned to a colour almost like the backing of mirrors, and then, with the boy's aid, hoisted her aboard, the male fish had stayed by the side of the boat. Then, while the old man was clearing the lines and preparing the harpoon, the male fish jumped high into the air beside the boat to see where the female was and then went down deep, his lavender wings, that were his pectoral fins, spread wide and all his wide lavender stripes showing. He was beautiful, the old man remembered, and he had stayed. That was the saddest thing I ever saw with them, the old man thought. The boy was sad too and we begged her pardon and butchered her promptly.

"I wish the boy was here," he said aloud and settled himself against the rounded planks of the bow and felt the strength of the great fish through the line he held across his shoulders moving steadily toward whatever he had chosen.

When once, through my treachery, it had been necessary to him to make a choice, the old man thought. His choice had been to stay in the deep dark water far out beyond all snares and traps and treacheries. My choice was to go there to find him beyond all people. Beyond all people in the world. Now we are joined together and have been since noon. And no one to help either one of us. Perhaps I should not have been a fisherman, he thought. But that was the thing that I was born for. I must surely remember to eat the tuna after it gets light.

Chapter 11
Tug-of-War

Some time before daylight something took one of the baits that were behind him. He heard the stick break and the line begin to rush out over the gunwale of the skiff. In the darkness he loosened his sheath knife and taking all the strain of the fish on his left shoulder he leaned back and cut the line against the wood of the gunwale. Then he cut the other line closest to him and in the dark made the loose ends of the reserve coils fast. He worked skillfully with the one hand and put his foot on the coils to hold them as he drew his knots tight. Now he had six reserve coils of line. There were two from each bait he had severed and the two from the bait the fish had taken and they were all connected.

After it is light, he thought, I will work back to the forty-fathom bait and cut it away too and link up the reserve coils. I will have lost two hundred fathoms of good Catalan cardel and the hooks and leaders. That can be replaced. But who replaces this fish if I hook some fish and it cuts him off? I don't know what that fish was that took the bait just now. It could have been a marlin or a broadbill or a shark. I never felt him. I had to get rid of him too fast.

Aloud he said, "I wish I had the boy."
But you haven't got the boy, he thought. You have only

yourself and you had better work back to the last line now, in the dark or not in the dark, and cut it away and hook up the two reserve coils. So he did it. It was difficult in the dark and once the fish made a surge that pulled him down on his face and made a cut below his eye. The blood ran down his cheek a little way. But it coagulated and dried before it reached his chin and he worked his way back to the bow and rested against the wood.

He adjusted the sack and carefully worked the line so that it came across a new part of his shoulders and, holding it anchored with his shoulders, he carefully felt the pull of the fish and then felt with his hand the progress of the skiff through the water.

I wonder what he made that lurch for, he thought. The wire must have slipped on the great hill of his back. Certainly his back cannot feel as badly as mine does. But he cannot pull this skiff forever, no matter how great he is. Now everything is cleared away that might make trouble and I have a big reserve of line; all that a man can ask.

"Fish," he said softly, aloud, "I'll stay with you until I am dead."

He'll stay with me too, I suppose, the old man thought and he waited for it to be light. It was cold now in the time before daylight and he pushed against the wood to be warm. I can do it as long as he can, he thought. And in the first light the line extended out and down into the water.

The boat moved steadily and when the first edge of the sun rose it was on the old man's right shoulder.

"He's headed north," the old man said. The current will have set us far to the eastward, he thought. I wish he would turn with the current. That would show that he was tiring. When the sun had risen further the old man realized that the fish was not tiring. There was only one favorable sign. The slant of the line showed he was swimming at a lesser depth. That did not necessarily mean that he would jump. But he might.

"God let him jump," the old man said. "I have enough line to handle him."

Maybe if I can increase the tension just a little it will hurt him and he will jump, he thought. Now that it is daylight let him jump so that he'll fill the sacks along his backbone with air and then he cannot go deep to die.

He tried to increase the tension, but the line had been taut up to the very edge of the breaking point since he had hooked the fish and he felt the harshness as he leaned back to pull and knew he could put no more strain on it. I must not jerk it ever, he thought. Each jerk widens the cut the hook makes and then when he does jump he might throw it. Anyway I feel better with the sun and for once I do not have to look into it.

There was yellow weed on the line but the old man knew

that only made an added drag and he was pleased. It was the yellow Gulf weed that had made so much phosphorescence in the night.

"Fish," he said, "I love you and respect you very much. But I will kill you dead before this day ends." Let us hope so, he thought.

Chapter 12
A Small Bird

A small bird came toward the skiff from the north. He was a warbler and flying very low over the water. The old man could see that he was very tired. The bird made the stern of the boat and rested there. Then he flew around the old man's head and rested on the line where he was more comfortable.

"How old are you?" the old man asked the bird. "Is this your first trip?"

The bird looked at him when he spoke. He was too tired even to examine the line and he teetered on it as his delicate feet gripped it fast.

"It's steady," the old man told him. "It's too steady. You shouldn't be that tired after a windless night. What are birds coming to?"

The hawks, he thought, that come out to sea to meet them. But he said nothing of this to the bird who could not understand him anyway and who would learn about the hawks soon enough.

"Take a good rest, small bird," he said. "Then go in and take your chance like any man or bird or fish."

It encouraged him to talk because his back had stiffened in the night and it hurt truly now.

"Stay at my house if you like, bird," he said. "I am sorry I cannot hoist the sail and take you in with the small breeze that is rising. But I am with a friend."

Just then the fish gave a sudden lurch that pulled the old man down onto the bow and would have pulled him overboard if he had not braced himself and given some line. The bird had flown up when the line jerked and the old man had not even seen him go.

He felt the line carefully with his right hand and noticed his hand was bleeding.

"Something hurt him then," he said aloud and pulled back on the line to see if he could turn the fish. But when he was touching the breaking point he held steady and settled back against the strain of the line.

"You're feeling it now, fish," he said. "And so, God knows, am I."

He looked around for the bird now because he would

have liked him for company. The bird was gone. You did not stay long, the man thought. But it is rougher where you are going until you make the shore.

How did I let the fish cut me with that one quick pull he made? I must be getting very stupid. Or perhaps I was looking at the small bird and thinking of him. Now I will pay attention to my work and then I must eat the tuna so that I will not have a failure of strength.

"I wish the boy were here and that I had some salt," he said aloud.

Chapter 13
Left Hand

Shifting the weight of the line to his left shoulder and kneeling carefully he washed his hand in the ocean and held it there, submerged, for more than a minute watching the blood trail away and the steady movement of the water against his hand as the boat moved.

"He has slowed much," he said.

The old man would have liked to keep his hand in the salt water longer but he was afraid of another sudden lurch by the fish and he stood up and braced himself and held his hand up against the sun. It was only a line burn that had cut his flesh. But it was in the working part of his hand. He knew he would need his hands before this was over and he did not like to be cut before it started.

"Now," he said, when his hand had dried, "I must eat the small tuna. I can reach him with the gaff and eat him here in comfort."

He knelt down and found the tuna under the stem with the gaff and drew it toward him keeping it clear of the coiled lines. Holding the line with his left shoulder again, and bracing on his left hand and arm, he took the tuna off the gaff hook and put the gaff back in place. He put one knee on the fish and cut strips of dark red meat longitudinally from the back of the head to the tail. They were wedge-shaped strips and he cut them from next to the back bone down to the edge of the belly. When he had cut six strips he spread them out on the wood of the bow, wiped his knife on his trousers, and lifted the carcass of the bonito by the tail and dropped it overboard.

"I don't think I can eat an entire one," he said and drew his knife across one of the strips. He could feel the steady hard pull of the line and his left hand was cramped. It drew up tight on the heavy cord and he looked at it in disgust.

"What kind of a hand is that," he said. "Cramp then if you want. Make yourself into a claw. It will do you no good."

Come on, he thought and looked down into the dark water at the slant of the line. Eat it now and it will strengthen the hand. It is not the hand's fault and you have been many hours with the fish. But you can stay with him forever. Eat the bonito now. He picked up a piece and put it in his mouth and chewed it slowly. It was not unpleasant. Chew it well, he thought, and get all the juices. It would not be had to eat with a little lime or with lemon or with salt.

"How do you feel, hand?" he asked the cramped hand that was almost as stiff as rigor mortis. "I'll eat some more for you."

He ate the other part of the piece that he had cut in two. He chewed it carefully and then spat out the skin.

"How does it go, hand? Or is it too early to know?" He took another full piece and chewed it.

"It is a strong full-blooded fish," he thought. "I was lucky to get him instead of dolphin. Dolphin is too sweet. This is hardly sweet at all and all the strength is still in it."

There is no sense in being anything but practical though, he thought. I wish I had some salt. And I do not know whether the sun will rot or dry what is left, so I had better eat it all although I am not hungry. The fish is calm and steady. I will eat it all and then I will be ready.

"Be patient, hand," he said. "I do this for you."

I wish I could feed the fish, he thought. He is my brother. But I must kill him and keep strong to do it. Slowly and conscientiously he ate all of the wedge-shaped strips of fish. He straightened up, wiping his hand on his trousers.

"Now," he said. "You can let the cord go, hand, and I will handle him with the right arm alone until you stop that nonsense."

He put his left foot on the heavy line that the left hand had held and lay back against the pull against his back.

"God help me to have the cramp go," he said. "Because I do not know what the fish is going to do."

But he seems calm, he thought, and following his plan. But what is his plan, he thought. And what is mine? Mine I must improvise to his because of his great size. If he will jump I can kill him. But he stays down forever. Then I will stay down with him forever.

He rubbed the cramped hand against his trousers and tried to gentle the fingers. But it would not open. Maybe it will open with the sun, he thought. Maybe it will open when the strong raw tuna is digested. If I have to have it, I will open it, cost whatever it costs. But I do not want to open it now by force. Let it open by itself and come back of its own accord. After all I abused it much in the night when it was necessary to free and untie the various lines.

Chapter 14
Jumping Up

He looked across the sea and knew how alone he was now. But he could see the prisms in the deep dark water and the line stretching ahead and the strange undulation of the calm. The clouds were building up now for the trade wind and he looked ahead and saw a flight of wild ducks etching themselves against the sky over the water, then blurring, then etching again and he knew no man was ever alone on the sea.

He thought of how some men feared being out of sight of land in a small boat and knew they were right in the months of sudden bad weather. But now they were in hurricane months and, when there are no hurricanes, the weather of hurricane months is the best of all the year.

If there is a hurricane you always see the signs of it in the sky for days ahead, if you are at sea. They do not see it ashore because they do not know what to look for, he thought. The land must make a difference too, in the shape of the clouds. But we have no hurricane coming now.

He looked at the sky and saw the white cumulus built like friendly piles of ice cream and high above were the thin feathers of the cirrus against the high September sky.

"Light **brisa**," he said. "Better weather for me than for you, fish."

His left hand was still cramped, but he was unknotting it slowly. I hate a cramp, he thought. It is a treachery of one's own body. It is humiliating before others to have a diarrhoea from ptomaine poisoning or to vomit from it. But a cramp, he thought of it as a ***calambre***, humiliates oneself especially when one is alone.

If the boy were here he could rub it for me and loosen it down from the forearm, he thought. But it will loosen up.

Then, with his right hand he felt the difference in the pull of the line before he saw the slant change in the water. Then, as he leaned against the line and slapped his left hand hard and fast against his thigh he saw the line slanting slowly upward.

"He's coming up," he said. "Come on hand. Please come on."

The line rose slowly and steadily and then the surface of the ocean bulged ahead of the boat and the fish came out. He came out unendingly and water poured from his sides. He was bright in the sun and his head and back were dark purple and in the sun the stripes on his sides showed wide and a light lavender. His sword was as long as a baseball bat and tapered like a rapier and he rose his full length from the water and then re-entered it, smoothly, like a diver and the old man saw the great scythe-blade of his tail go under and the line commenced to race out.

"He is two feet longer than the skiff," the old man said. The line was going out fast but steadily and the fish was not panicked. The old man was trying with both hands to keep the line just inside of breaking strength. He knew that if he could not slow the fish with a steady pressure the fish could take out all the line and break it.

He is a great fish and I must convince him, he thought. I must never let him learn his strength nor what he could do if he made his run. If I were him I would put in everything now and go until something broke. But, thank God, they are not as intelligent as we who kill them; although they are more noble and more able.

The old man had seen many great fish. He had seen many that weighed more than a thousand pounds and he had caught two of that size in his life, but never alone. Now alone, and out of sight of land, he was fast to the biggest fish that he had ever seen and bigger than he had ever heard of, and his left hand was still as tight as the gripped claws of an eagle.

It will uncramp though, he thought. Surely it will uncramp to help my right hand. There are three things that are brothers: the fish and my two hands. It must uncramp. It is unworthy of it to be cramped. The fish had slowed again and was going at his usual pace.

I wonder why he jumped, the old man thought. He jumped almost as though to show me how big he was. I know now, anyway, he thought. I wish I could show him what sort of man I am. But then he would see the cramped hand. Let him think I am more man than I am and I will be so. I wish I was the fish, he thought, with everything he has against only my will and my intelligence.

Chapter 15
The Prayer

He settled comfortably against the wood and took his suffering as it came and the fish swam steadily and the boat moved slowly through the dark water. There was a small sea rising with the wind coming up from the east and at noon the old man's left hand was uncramped.

"Bad news for you, fish," he said and shifted the line over the sacks that covered his shoulders.

He was comfortable but suffering, although he did not admit the suffering at all.

"I am not religious," he said. "But I will say ten Our Fathers and ten Hail Marys that I should catch this fish, and I promise to make a pilgrimage to the Virgin of Cobre if I catch him. That is a promise."

He commenced to say his prayers mechanically. Sometimes he would be so tired that he could not remember the prayer and then he would say them fast so that they would come automatically. Hail Marys are easier to say than Our Fathers, he thought.

"Hail Mary full of Grace the Lord is with thee. Blessed art

thou among women and blessed is the fruit of thy womb, Jesus. Holy Mary, Mother of God, pray for us sinners now and at the hour of our death. Amen."

Then he added, "Blessed Virgin, pray for the death of this fish. Wonderful though he is."

With his prayers said, and feeling much better, but suffering exactly as much, and perhaps a little more, he leaned against the wood of the bow and began, mechanically, to work the fingers of his left hand. The sun was hot now although the breeze was rising gently.

"I had better re-bait that little line out over the stern," he said. "If the fish decides to stay another night I will need to eat again and the water is low in the bottle. I don't think I can get anything but a dolphin here. But if I eat him fresh enough he won't be bad. I wish a flying fish would come on board tonight. But I have no light to attract them. A flying fish is excellent to eat raw and I would not have to cut him up. I must save all my strength now. Christ, I did not know he was so big."

"I'll kill him though," he said. "In all his greatness and his glory." Although it is unjust, he thought. But I will show him what a man can do and what a man endures.

"I told the boy I was a strange old man," he said. "Now is when I must prove it." The thousand times that he had proved it meant nothing. Now he was proving it again. Each time was a new time and he never thought about the past when he was doing it.

I wish he'd sleep and I could sleep and dream about the lions, he thought. Why are the lions the main thing that is left? Don't think, old man, he said to himself, Rest gently now against the wood and think of nothing. He is working. Work as little as you can.

It was getting into the afternoon and the boat still moved slowly and steadily. But there was an added drag now from the easterly breeze and the old man rode gently with the small sea and the hurt of the cord across his back came to him easily and smoothly.

Once in the afternoon the line started to rise again. But the fish only continued to swim at a slightly higher level. The sun was on the old man's left arm and shoulder and on his back. So he knew the fish had turned east of north.

Now that he had seen him once, he could picture the fish swimming in the water with his purple pectoral fins set wide as wings and the great erect tail slicing through the dark. I wonder how much he sees at that depth, the old man thought. His eye is huge and a horse, with much less eye, can see in the dark. Once I could see quite well in the dark. Not in the absolute dark. But almost as a cat sees.

The sun and his steady movement of his fingers had uncramped his left hand now completely and he began to shift more of the strain to it and he shrugged the muscles of his back to shift the hurt of the cord a little.

"If you're not tired, fish," he said aloud, "you must be very strange."

He felt very tired now and he knew the night would come soon and he tried to think of other things. He thought of the Big Leagues, to him they were the **Gran Ligas**, and he knew that the Yankees of New York were playing the Tigers of Detroit.

This is the second day now that I do not know the result of the juegos, he thought. But I must have confidence and I must be worthy of the great DiMaggio who does all things perfectly even with the pain of the bone spur in his heel. What is a bone spur? he asked himself. **Un espuela de hueso**. We do not have them. Can it be as painful as the spur of a fighting cock in one's heel? I do not think I could endure that or the loss of the eye and of both eyes and continue to fight as the fighting cocks do. Man is not much beside the great birds and beasts. Still I would rather be that beast down there in the darkness of the sea. "Unless sharks come," he said aloud. "If sharks come, God pity him and me."

Do you believe the great DiMaggio would stay with a fish as long as I will stay with this one? he thought. I am sure he would and more since he is young and strong. Also his father was a fisherman. But would the bone spur hurt him too much? "I do not know," he said aloud. "I never had a bone spur."

Chapter 16
Arm Wrestling

As the sun set he remembered, to give himself more confidence, the time in the tavern at Casablanca when he had played the hand game with the great black man from Cienfuegos who was the strongest man on the docks.

They had gone one day and one night with their elbows on a chalk line on the table and their forearms straight up and their hands gripped tight. Each one was trying to force the other's hand down onto the table. There was much betting and people went in and out of the room under the kerosene lights and he had looked at the arm and hand of the black man and at the black man's face.

They changed the referees every four hours after the first eight so that the referees could sleep. Blood came out from under the fingernails of both his and the negro's hands and they looked each other in the eye and at their hands and forearms and the bettors went in and out of the room and sat on high chairs against the wall and watched. The walls were painted bright blue and were of wood and the lamps threw their shadows against them. The negro's shadow was huge and it moved on the wall as the breeze moved the lamps.

The odds would change back and forth all night and they fed the black man rum and lighted cigarettes for him. Then the black man, after the rum, would try for a tremendous effort and once he had the old man, who was not an old man then but was Santiago **El Campeon**, nearly three inches off balance. But the old man had raised his hand up to dead even again. He was sure then that he had the black man, who was a fine man and a great athlete, beaten.

And at daylight when the bettors were asking that it be called a draw and the referee was shaking his head, he had unleashed his effort and forced the hand of the negro down and down until it rested on the wood.

The match had started on a Sunday morning and ended on a Monday morning. Many of the bettors had asked for a draw because they had to go to work on the docks loading sacks of sugar or at the Havana Coal Company. Otherwise everyone would have wanted it to go to a finish. But he had finished it anyway and before anyone had to go to work.

For a long time after that everyone had called him The Champion and there had been a return match in the spring. But not much money was bet and he had won it quite easily since he had broken the confidence of the black man from Cienfuegos in the first match.

After that he had a few matches and then no more. He decided that he could beat anyone if he wanted to badly enough and he decided that it was bad for his right hand for fishing. He had tried a few practice matches with his left hand. But his left hand had always been a traitor and would not do what he called on it to do and he did not trust it.

The sun will bake it out well now, he thought. It should not cramp on me again unless it gets too cold in the night. I wonder what this night will bring.

An airplane passed overhead on its course to Miami and he watched its shadow scaring up the schools of flying fish.
"With so much flying fish there should be dolphin," he said, and leaned back on the line to see if it was possible to gain any on his fish. But he could not and it stayed at the hardness and water-drop shivering that preceded breaking. The boat moved ahead slowly and he watched the airplane until he could no longer see it.

It must be very strange in an airplane, he thought. I wonder what the sea looks like from that height? They should be able to see the fish well if they do not fly too high. I would like to fly very slowly at two hundred fathoms high and see the fish from above.

In the turtle boats I was in the cross-trees of the mast-head and even at that height I saw much. The dolphin look greener from there and you can see their stripes and their purple spots and you can see all of the school as they swim. Why is it that all the fast-moving fish of the dark current have purple backs and usually purple stripes or spots? The dolphin looks green of course because he is really golden. But when he comes to feed, truly hungry, purple stripes show on his sides as on a marlin. Can it be anger, or the greater speed he makes that brings them out?

Chapter 17
The Dolphin

Just before it was dark, as they passed a great island of Sargasso weed that heaved and swung in the light sea as though the ocean were making love with something under a yellow blanket, his small line was taken by a dolphin. He saw it first when it jumped in the air, true gold in the last of the sun and bending and flapping wildly in the air. It jumped again and again in the acrobatics of its fear and he worked his way back to the stern and crouching and holding the big line with his right hand and arm, he pulled the dolphin in with his left hand, stepping on the gained line each time with his bare left foot.

When the fish was at the stem, plunging and cutting from side to side in desperation, the old man leaned over the stern and lifted the burnished gold fish with its purple spots over the stem. Its jaws were working convulsively in quick bites against the hook and it pounded the bottom of the skiff with its long flat body, its tail and its head until he clubbed it across the shining golden head until it shivered and was still.

The old man unhooked the fish, re-baited the line with another sardine and tossed it over. Then he worked his way slowly back to the bow. He washed his left hand and wiped it on his trousers. Then he shifted the heavy line from his right hand to his left and washed his right hand in the sea while he watched the sun go into the ocean and the slant of the big cord.

"He hasn't changed at all," he said. But watching the movement of the water against his hand he noticed that it was perceptibly slower.

"I'll lash the two oars together across the stern and that will slow him in the night," he said. "He's good for the night and so am I."

It would be better to gut the dolphin a little later to save the blood in the meat, he thought. I can do that a little later and lash the oars to make a drag at the same time. I had better keep the fish quiet now and not disturb him too much at sunset. The setting of the sun is a difficult time for all fish.

He let his hand dry in the air then grasped the line with it and eased himself as much as he could and allowed himself to be pulled forward against the wood so that the boat took the strain as much, or more, than he did.

I'm learning how to do it, he thought. This part of it anyway. Then too, remember he hasn't eaten since he took the bait and he is huge and needs much food. I have eaten the whole bonito. Tomorrow I will eat the dolphin. He called it **dorado**. Perhaps I should eat some of it when I clean it. It will be harder to eat than the bonito. But, then, nothing is easy.

"How do you feel, fish?" he asked aloud. "I feel good and my left hand is better and I have food for a night and a day. Pull the boat, fish."

He did not truly feel good because the pain from the cord across his back had almost passed pain and gone into a dullness that he mistrusted. But I have had worse things than that, he thought. My hand is only cut a little and the cramp is gone from the other. My legs are all right. Also now I have gained on him in the question of sustenance.

It was dark now as it becomes dark quickly after the sun sets in September. He lay against the worn wood of the bow and rested all that he could. The first stars were out. He did not know the name of Rigel but he saw it and knew soon they would all be out and he would have all his distant friends.

"The fish is my friend too," he said aloud. "I have never seen or heard of such a fish. But I must kill him. I am glad we do not have to try to kill the stars."

Imagine if each day a man must try to kill the moon, he thought. The moon runs away. But imagine if a man each day should have to try to kill the sun? We were born lucky, he thought.

Then he was sorry for the great fish that had nothing to eat and his determination to kill him never relaxed in his sorrow for him. How many people will he feed, he thought. But are they worthy to eat him? No, of course not. There is no one worthy of eating him from the manner of his behaviour and his great dignity.

I do not understand these things, he thought. But it is good that we do not have to try to kill the sun or the moon or the stars. It is enough to live on the sea and kill our true brothers.

Now, he thought, I must think about the drag. It has its perils and its merits. I may lose so much line that I will lose him, if he makes his effort and the drag made by the oars is in place and the boat loses all her lightness. Her lightness prolongs both our suffering but it is my safety since he has great speed that he has never yet employed. No matter what passes I must gut the dolphin so he does not spoil and eat some of him to be strong.

Now I will rest an hour more and feel that he is solid and steady before I move back to the stern to do the work and make the decision. In the meantime I can see how he acts and if he shows any changes. The oars are a good trick; but it has reached the time to play for safety. He is much fish still and I saw that the hook was in the corner of his mouth and he has kept his mouth tight shut. The punishment of the hook is nothing. The punishment of hunger, and that he is against something that he does not comprehend, is everything. Rest now, old man, and let him work until your next duty comes.

Chapter 18
Sleep

He rested for what he believed to be two hours. The moon did not rise now until late and he had no way of judging the time. Nor was he really resting except comparatively. He was still bearing the pull of the fish across his shoulders but he placed his left hand on the gunwale of the bow and confided more and more of the resistance to the fish to the skiff itself.

How simple it would be if I could make the line fast, he thought. But with one small lurch he could break it. I must cushion the pull of the line with my body and at all times be ready to give line with both hands.

"But you have not slept yet, old man," he said aloud. "It is half a day and a night and now another day and you have not slept. You must devise a way so that you sleep a little if he is quiet and steady. If you do not sleep you might become unclear in the head."

I'm clear enough in the head, he thought. Too clear. I am as clear as the stars that are my brothers. Still I must sleep. They sleep and the moon and the sun sleep and even the ocean sleeps sometimes on certain days when there is no current and a flat calm. But remember to sleep, he thought. Make yourself do it and devise some simple and sure way about the lines.

Now go back and prepare the dolphin. It is too dangerous to rig the oars as a drag if you must sleep. I could go without sleeping, he told himself. But it would be too dangerous.

He started to work his way back to the stern on his hands and knees, being careful not to jerk against the fish. He may be half asleep himself, he thought. But I do not want him to rest. He must pull until he dies.

Back in the stern he turned so that his left hand held the strain of the line across his shoulders and drew his knife from its sheath with his right hand. The stars were bright now and he saw the dolphin clearly and he pushed the blade of his knife into his head and drew him out from under the stern. He put one of his feet on the fish and slit him quickly from the vent up to the tip of his lower jaw. Then he put his knife down and gutted him with his right hand, scooping him clean and pulling the gills clear. He felt the maw heavy and slippery in his hands and he slit it open. There were two flying fish inside. They were fresh and hard and he laid them side by side and dropped the guts and the gills over the stern. They sank leaving a trail of phosphorescence in the water. The dolphin was cold and a leprous gray-white now in the starlight and the old man skinned one side of him while he held his right foot on the fish's head. Then he turned him over and skinned the other side and cut each side off from the head down to the tail.

He slid the carcass overboard and looked to see if there was any swirl in the water. But there was only the light of its slow descent. He turned then and placed the two flying fish inside the two fillets of fish and putting his knife back in its sheath, he worked his way slowly back to the bow. His back was bent with the weight of the line across it and he carried the fish in his right hand.

Back in the bow he laid the two fillets of fish out on the wood with the flying fish beside them. After that he settled the line across his shoulders in a new place and held it again with his left hand resting on the gunwale. Then he leaned over the side and washed the flying fish in the water, noting the speed of the water against his hand. His hand was phosphorescent from skinning the fish and he watched the flow of the water against it. The flow was less strong and as he rubbed the side of his hand against the planking of the skiff, particles of phosphorus floated off and drifted slowly astern.

"He is tiring or he is resting," the old man said. "Now let me get through the eating of this dolphin and get some rest and a little sleep."

Under the stars and with the night colder all the time he ate half of one of the dolphin fillets and one of the flying fish, gutted and with its head cut off.

"What an excellent fish dolphin is to eat cooked," he said. "And what a miserable fish raw. I will never go in a boat again without salt or limes."

If I had brains I would have splashed water on the bow all day and drying, it would have made salt, he thought. But then I did not hook the dolphin until almost sunset. Still it was a lack of preparation. But I have chewed it all well and I am not nauseated.

The sky was clouding over to the east and one after another the stars he knew were gone. It looked now as though he were moving into a great canyon of clouds and the wind had dropped.

"There will be bad weather in three or four days," he said. "But not tonight and not tomorrow. Rig now to get some sleep, old man, while the fish is calm and steady."

He held the line tight in his right hand and then pushed his thigh against his right hand as he leaned all his weight against the wood of the bow. Then he passed the line a little lower on his shoulders and braced his left hand on it.

My right hand can hold it as long as it is braced, he thought. If it relaxes in sleep my left hand will wake me as the line goes out. It is hard on the right hand. But he is used to punishment. Even if I sleep twenty minutes or a half an hour it is good. He lay forward cramping himself against the line with all of his body, putting all his weight onto his right band, and he was asleep.

Chapter 19
A Cut on the Hand

He did not dream of the lions but instead of a vast school of porpoises that stretched for eight or ten miles and it was in the time of their mating and they would leap high into the air and return into the same hole they had made in the water when they leaped. Then he dreamed that he was in the village on his bed and there was a norther and he was very cold and his right arm was asleep because his head had rested on it instead of a pillow.

After that he began to dream of the long yellow beach and he saw the first of the lions come down onto it in the early dark and then the other lions came and he rested his chin on the wood of the bows where the ship lay anchored with the evening off-shore breeze and he waited to see if there would be more lions and he was happy.

The moon had been up for a long time but he slept on and the fish pulled on steadily and the boat moved into the tunnel of clouds.

He woke with the jerk of his right fist coming up against his face and the line burning out through his right hand. He had no feeling of his left hand but he braked all he could with his right and the line rushed out. Finally his left hand found the line and he leaned back against the line and now it burned his back and his left hand, and his left hand was taking all the strain and cutting badly.

He looked back at the coils of line and they were feeding smoothly. Just then the fish jumped making a great bursting of the ocean and then a heavy fall. Then he jumped again and again and the boat was going fast although line was still racing out and the old man was raising the strain to breaking point and raising it to breaking point again and again. He had been pulled down tight onto the bow and his face was in the cut slice of dolphin and he could not move.

This is what we waited for, he thought. So now let us take it. Make him pay for the line, he thought. Make him pay for it.

He could not see the fish's jumps but only heard the breaking of the ocean and the heavy splash as he fell. The speed of the line was cutting his hands badly but he had always known this would happen and he tried to keep the cutting across the calloused parts and not let the line slip into the palm nor cut the fingers.

If the boy was here he would wet the coils of line, he thought. Yes. If the boy were here. If the boy were here.

The line went out and out and out but it was slowing now and he was making the fish earn each inch of it.

Now he got his head up from the wood and out of the slice of fish that his cheek had crushed. Then he was on his knees and then he rose slowly to his feet. He was ceding line but more slowly all the time. He worked back to where he could feel with his foot the coils of line that he could not see. There was plenty of line still and now the fish had to pull the friction of all that new line through the water.

Yes, he thought. And now he has jumped more than a dozen times and filled the sacks along his back with air and he cannot go down deep to die where I cannot bring him up. He will start circling soon and then I must work on him. I wonder what started him so suddenly? Could it have been hunger that made him desperate, or was he frightened by something in the night? Maybe he suddenly felt fear. But he was such a calm, strong fish and he seemed so fearless and so confident. It is strange.

"You better be fearless and confident yourself, old man," he said. "You're holding him again but you cannot get line. But soon he has to circle."

The old man held him with his left hand and his shoulders now and stooped down and scooped up water in his right hand to get the crushed dolphin flesh off of his face. He was afraid that it might nauseate him and he would vomit and lose his strength.

When his face was cleaned he washed his right hand in the water over the side and then let it stay in the salt water while he watched the first light come before the sunrise. He's headed almost east, he thought. That means he is tired and going with the current. Soon he will have to circle. Then our true work begins.

After he judged that his right hand had been in the water long enough he took it out and looked at it.

"It is not bad," he said. "And pain does not matter to a man."

He took hold of the line carefully so that it did not fit into any of the fresh line cuts and shifted his weight so that he could put his left hand into the sea on the other side of the skiff.

"You did not do so badly for something worthless," he said to his left hand. "But there was a moment when I could not find you."

Why was I not born with two good hands? he thought. Perhaps it was my fault in not training that one properly. But God knows he has had enough chances to learn. He did not do so badly in the night, though, and he has only cramped once. If he cramps again let the line cut him off.

When he thought that he knew that he was not being clear-headed and he thought he should chew some more of the dolphin. But I can't, he told himself. It is better to be light-headed than to lose your strength from nausea. And I know I cannot keep it if I eat it since my face was in it. I will keep it for an emergency until it goes bad. But it is too late to try for strength now through nourishment. You're stupid, he told himself. Eat the other flying fish.

It was there, cleaned and ready, and he picked it up with his left hand and ate it chewing the bones carefully and eating all of it down to the tail. It has more nourishment than almost any fish, he thought. At least the kind of strength that I need. Now I have done what I can, he thought. Let him begin to circle and let the fight come.

Chapter 20
Circle

The sun was rising for the third time since he had put to sea when the fish started to circle.

He could not see by the slant of the line that the fish was circling. It was too early for that. He just felt a faint slackening of the pressure of the line and he commenced to pull on it gently with his right hand. It tightened, as always, but just when he reached the point where it would break, line began to come in.

He slipped his shoulders and head from under the line and began to pull in line steadily and gently. He used both of his hands in a swinging motion and tried to do the pulling as much as he could with his body and his legs. His old legs and shoulders pivoted with the swinging of the pulling.

"It is a very big circle," he said. "But he is circling." Then the line would not come in any more and he held it until he saw the drops jumping from it in the sun. Then it started out and the old man knelt down and let it go grudgingly back into the dark water.

"He is making the far part of his circle now," he said. I must hold all I can, he thought. The strain will shorten his circle each time. Perhaps in an hour I will see him. Now I must convince him and then I must kill him.

But the fish kept on circling slowly and the old man was wet with sweat and tired deep into his bones two hours later. But the circles were much shorter now and from the way the line slanted he could tell the fish had risen steadily while he swam.

For an hour the old man had been seeing black spots before his eyes and the sweat salted his eyes and salted the cut over his eye and on his forehead. He was not afraid of the black spots. They were normal at the tension that he was pulling on the line. Twice, though, he had felt faint and dizzy and that had worried him.

"I could not fail myself and die on a fish like this," he said. "Now that I have him coming so beautifully, God help me endure. I'll say a hundred Our Fathers and a hundred Hail Marys. But I cannot say them now.

Consider them said, he thought. I'll say them later. Just then he felt a sudden banging and jerking on the line he held with his two hands. It was sharp and hard-feeling and heavy.

He is hitting the wire leader with his spear, he thought. That was bound to come. He had to do that. It may make him jump though and I would rather he stayed circling now. The jumps were necessary for him to take air. But after that each one can widen the opening of the hook wound and he can throw the hook.

"Don't jump, fish," he said. "Don't jump."

The fish hit the wire several times more and each time he shook his head the old man gave up a little line.

I must hold his pain where it is, he thought. Mine does not matter. I can control mine. But his pain could drive him mad.

After a while the fish stopped beating at the wire and started circling slowly again. The old man was gaining line steadily now. But he felt faint again. He lifted some sea water with his left hand and put it on his head. Then he put more on and rubbed the back of his neck.

"I have no cramps," he said. "He'll be up soon and I can last. You have to last. Don't even speak of it."

He kneeled against the bow and, for a moment, slipped the line over his back again. I'll rest now while he goes out on the circle and then stand up and work on him when he comes in, he decided.

It was a great temptation to rest in the bow and let the

fish make one circle by himself without recovering any line. But when the strain showed the fish had turned to come toward the boat, the old man rose to his feet and started the pivoting and the weaving pulling that brought in all the line he gained.

I'm tireder than I have ever been, he thought, and now the trade wind is rising. But that will be good to take him in with. I need that badly.

"I'll rest on the next turn as he goes out," he said. "I feel much better. Then in two or three turns more I will have him."

His straw hat was far on the back of his head and he sank down into the bow with the pull of the line as he felt the fish turn.

You work now, fish, he thought. I'll take you at the turn. The sea had risen considerably. But it was a fair-weather breeze and he had to have it to get home.

"I'll just steer south and west," he said. "A man is never lost at sea and it is a long island."

Chapter 21
The Death of the Marlin

It was on the third turn that he saw the fish first. He saw him first as a dark shadow that took so long to pass under the boat that he could not believe its length.

"No," he said. "He can't be that big."

But he was that big and at the end of this circle he came to the surface only thirty yards away and the man saw his tail out of water. It was higher than a big scythe blade and a very pale lavender above the dark blue water. It raked back and as the fish swam just below the surface the old man could see his huge bulk and the purple stripes that banded him. His dorsal fin was down and his huge pectorals were spread wide.

On this circle the old man could see the fish's eye and the two gray sucking fish that swam around him. Sometimes they attached themselves to him. Sometimes they darted off. Sometimes they would swim easily in his shadow. They were each over three feet long and when they swam fast they lashed their whole bodies like eels.

The old man was sweating now but from something else besides the sun. On each calm placid turn the fish made he was gaining line and he was sure that in two turns more he would have a chance to get the harpoon in. But I must get him close, close, close, he thought. I mustn't try for the head. I must get the heart.

"Be calm and strong, old man," he said.

On the next circle the fish's back was out but he was a little too far from the boat. On the next circle he was still too far away but he was higher out of water and the old man was sure that by gaining some more line he could have him alongside.

He had rigged his harpoon long before and its coil of light rope was in a round basket and the end was made fast to the bitt in the bow.

The fish was coming in on his circle now calm and beautiful looking and only his great tail moving. The old man pulled on him all that he could to bring him closer. For just a moment the fish turned a little on his side. Then he straightened himself and began another circle.

"I moved him," the old man said. "I moved him then."

He felt faint again now but he held on the great fish all the strain that he could. I moved him, he thought. Maybe this time I can get him over. Pull, hands, he thought. Hold up, legs. Last for me, head. Last for me. You never went. This time I'll pull him over.

But when he put all of his effort on, starting it well out before the fish came alongside and pulling with all his strength, the fish pulled part way over and then righted himself and swam away.

"Fish," the old man said. "Fish, you are going to have to die anyway. Do you have to kill me too?"

That way nothing is accomplished, he thought. His mouth was too dry to speak but he could not reach for the water now. I must get him alongside this time, he thought. I am not good for many more turns. Yes you are, he told himself. You're good for ever.

On the next turn, he nearly had him. But again the fish righted himself and swam slowly away.

You are killing me, fish, the old man thought. But you have a right to. Never have I seen a greater, or more beautiful, or a calmer or more noble thing than you, brother. Come on and kill me. I do not care who kills who.

Now you are getting confused in the head, he thought. You must keep your head clear. Keep your head clear and know how to suffer like a man. Or a fish, he thought.

"Clear up, head," he said in a voice he could hardly hear. "Clear up."

Twice more it was the same on the turns. I do not know, the old man thought.

He had been on the point of feeling himself go each time. I do not know. But I will try it once more. He tried it once more and he felt himself going when he turned the fish. The fish righted himself and swam off again slowly with the great tail weaving in the air. I'll try it again, the old man promised, although his hands were mushy now and he could only see well in flashes. He tried it again and it was the same. So he thought, and he felt himself going before he started; I will try it once again.

He took all his pain and what was left of his strength and his long gone pride and he put it against the fish's agony and the fish came over onto his side and swam gently on his side, his bill almost touching the planking of the skiff and started to pass the boat, long, deep, wide, silver and barred with purple and interminable in the water.

The old man dropped the line and put his foot on it and lifted the harpoon as high as he could and drove it down with all his strength, and more strength he had just summoned, into the fish's side just behind the great chest fin that rose high in the air to the altitude of the man's chest. He felt the iron go in and he leaned on it and drove it further and then pushed all his weight after it.

Then the fish came alive, with his death in him, and rose high out of the water showing all his great length and width and all his power and his beauty. He seemed to hang in the air above the old man in the skiff. Then he fell into the water with a crash that sent spray over the old man and over all of the skiff.

The old man felt faint and sick and he could not see well. But he cleared the harpoon line and let it run slowly through his raw hands and, when he could see, he saw the fish was on his back with his silver belly up. The shaft of the harpoon was projecting at an angle from the fish's shoulder and the sea was discolouring with the red of the blood from his heart. First it was dark as a shoal in the blue water that was more than a mile deep. Then it spread like a cloud. The fish was silvery and still and floated with the waves.

Chapter 22
Tying the Marlin to the Boat

The old man looked carefully in the glimpse of vision that he had. Then he took two turns of the harpoon line around the bitt in the bow and hid his head on his hands.

"Keep my head dear," he said against the wood of the bow. "I am a tired old man. But I have killed this fish which is my brother and now I must do the slave work."

Now I must prepare the nooses and the rope to lash him alongside, he thought. Even if we were two and swamped her to load him and bailed her out, this skiff would never hold him. I must prepare everything, then bring him in and lash him well and step the mast and set sail for home.

He started to pull the fish in to have him alongside so that he could pass a line through his gills and out his mouth and make his head fast alongside the bow. I want to see him, he thought, and to touch and to feel him. He is my fortune, he thought. But that is not why I wish to feel him. I think I felt his heart, he thought. When I pushed on the harpoon shaft the second time. Bring him in now and make him fast and get the noose around his tail and another around his middle to bind him to the skiff.

"Get to work, old man," he said. He took a very small drink of the water. "There is very much slave work to be done now that the fight is over."

He looked up at the sky and then out to his fish. He looked at the sun carefully. It is not much more than noon, he thought. And the trade wind is rising. The lines all mean nothing now. The boy and I will splice them when we are home.

"Come on, fish," he said. But the fish did not come. Instead

he lay there wallowing now in the seas and the old man pulled the skiff up onto him.

When he was even with him and had the fish's head against the bow he could not believe his size. But he untied the harpoon rope from the bitt, passed it through the fish's gills and out his jaws, made a turn around his sword then passed the rope through the other gill, made another turn around the bill and knotted the double rope and made it fast to the bitt in the bow. He cut the rope then and went astern to noose the tail. The fish had turned silver from his original purple and silver, and the stripes showed the same pale violet colour as his tail. They were wider than a man's hand with his fingers spread and the fish's eye looked as detached as the mirrors in a periscope or as a saint in a procession.

"It was the only way to kill him," the old man said. He was feeling better since the water and he knew he would not go away and his head was clear. He's over fifteen hundred pounds the way he is, he thought. Maybe much more. If he dresses out two-thirds of that at thirty cents a pound?

"I need a pencil for that," he said. "My head is not that clear. But I think the great DiMaggio would be proud of me today. I had no bone spurs. But the hands and the back hurt truly." I wonder what a bone spur is, he thought. Maybe we have them without knowing of it.

He made the fish fast to bow and stern and to the middle thwart. He was so big it was like lashing a much bigger skiff alongside. He cut a piece of line and tied the fish's lower jaw against his bill so his mouth would not open and they would sail as cleanly as possible. Then he stepped the mast and, with the stick that was his gaff and with his boom rigged, the patched sail drew, the boat began to move, and half lying in the stern he sailed south-west.

He did not need a compass to tell him where southwest was. He only needed the feel of the trade wind and the drawing of the sail. I better put a small line out with a spoon on it and try and get something to eat and drink for the moisture. But he could not find a spoon and his sardines were rotten. So he hooked a patch of yellow Gulf weed with the gaff as they passed and shook it so that the small shrimps that were in it fell onto the planking of the skiff. There were more than a dozen of them and they jumped and kicked like sand fleas. The old man pinched their heads off with his thumb and forefinger and ate them chewing up the shells and the tails. They were very tiny but he knew they were nourishing and they tasted good.

The old man still had two drinks of water in the bottle and he used half of one after he had eaten the shrimps. The skiff was sailing well considering the handicaps and he steered with the tiller under his arm. He could see the fish and he had only to look at his hands and feel his back against the stern to know that this had truly happened and was not a dream. At one time when he was feeling so badly toward the end, he had thought perhaps it was a dream. Then when he had seen the fish come out of the water and hang motionless in the sky before he fell, he was sure there was some great strangeness and he could not believe it. Then he could not see well, although now he saw as well as ever.

Now he knew there was the fish and his hands and back were no dream. The hands cure quickly, he thought. I bled them clean and the salt water will heal them. The dark water of the true gulf is the greatest healer that there is. All I must do is keep the head clear. The hands have done their work and we sail well. With his mouth shut and his tail straight up and down we sail like brothers.

Then his head started to become a little unclear and he thought, is he bringing me in or am I bringing him in? If I were towing him behind there would be no question. Nor if the fish were in the skiff, with all dignity gone, there would be no question either. But they were sailing together lashed side by side and the old man thought, let him bring me in if it pleases him. I am only better than him through trickery and he meant me no harm.

Chapter 23
The Mako Shark

They sailed well and the old man soaked his hands in the salt water and tried to keep his head clear. There were high cumulus clouds and enough cirrus above them so that the old man knew the breeze would last all night. The old man looked at the fish constantly to make sure it was true. It was an hour before the first shark hit him.

The shark was not an accident. He had come up from deep down in the water as the dark cloud of blood had settled and dispersed in the mile deep sea. He had come up so fast and absolutely without caution that he broke the surface of the blue water and was in the sun. Then he fell back into the sea and picked up the scent and started swimming on the course the skiff and the fish had taken.

Sometimes he lost the scent. But he would pick it up again, or have just a trace of it, and he swam fast and hard on the course. He was a very big Mako shark built to swim as fast as the fastest fish in the sea and everything about him was beautiful except his jaws. His back was as blue as a sword fish's and his belly was silver and his hide was smooth and handsome. He was built as a sword fish except for his huge jaws which were tight shut now as he swam fast, just under the surface with his high dorsal fin knifing through the water without wavering. Inside the closed double lip of his jaws all of his eight rows of teeth were slanted inwards. They were not the ordinary pyramid-shaped teeth of most sharks. They were shaped like a man's fingers when they are crisped like claws. They were nearly as long as the fingers of the old man and they had razor-sharp cutting edges on both sides. This was a fish built to feed on all the fishes in the sea, that were so fast and strong and well armed that they had no other enemy. Now he speeded up as he smelled the fresher scent and his blue dorsal fin cut the water.

When the old man saw him coming he knew that this was a shark that had no fear at all and would do exactly what he wished. He prepared the harpoon and made the rope fast while he watched the shark come on. The rope was short as it lacked what he had cut away to lash the fish.

The old man's head was clear and good now and he was full of resolution but he had little hope. It was too good to last, he thought. He took one look at the great fish as he watched the shark close in. It might as well have been a dream, he thought. I cannot keep him from hitting me but maybe I can get him. **Dentuso**, he thought. Bad luck to your mother.

The shark closed fast astern and when he hit the fish the old man saw his mouth open and his strange eyes and the clicking chop of the teeth as he drove forward in the meat just above the tail. The shark's head was out of water and his back was coming out and the old man could hear the noise of skin and flesh ripping on the big fish when he rammed the harpoon down onto the shark's head at a spot where the line between his eyes intersected with the line that ran straight back from his nose. There were no such lines. There was only the heavy sharp blue head and the big eyes and the clicking, thrusting all-swallowing jaws. But that was the location of the brain and the old man hit it. He hit it with his blood mushed hands driving a good harpoon with all his strength. He hit it without hope but with resolution and complete malignancy.

The shark swung over and the old man saw his eye was

not alive and then he swung over once again, wrapping himself in two loops of the rope. The old man knew that he was dead but the shark would not accept it. Then, on his back, with his tail lashing and his jaws clicking, the shark plowed over the water as a speedboat does. The water was white where his tail beat it and three-quarters of his body was clear above the water when the rope came taut, shivered, and then snapped. The shark lay quietly for a little while on the surface and the old man watched him. Then he went down very slowly.

"He took about forty pounds," the old man said aloud. He took my harpoon too and all the rope, he thought, and now my fish bleeds again and there will be others. He did not like to look at the fish anymore since he had been mutilated. When the fish had been hit it was as though he himself were hit. But I killed the shark that hit my fish, he thought. And he was the biggest **dentuso** that I have ever seen. And God knows that I have seen big ones.

It was too good to last, he thought. I wish it had been a dream now and that I had never hooked the fish and was alone in bed on the newspapers.

"But man is not made for defeat," he said. "A man can be destroyed but not defeated." I am sorry that I killed the fish though, he thought. Now the bad time is coming and I do not even have the harpoon. The **dentuso** is cruel and able and strong and intelligent. But I was more intelligent than he was. Perhaps not, he thought. Perhaps I was only better armed.

"Don't think, old man," he said aloud. "Sail on this course and take it when it comes.

But I must think, he thought. Because it is all I have left. That and baseball. I wonder how the great DiMaggio would have liked the way I hit him in the brain? It was no great thing, he thought. Any man could do it. But do you think my hands were as great a handicap as the bone spurs? I cannot know. I never had anything wrong with my heel except the time the sting ray stung it when I stepped on him when swimming and paralyzed the lower leg and made the unbearable pain.

"Think about something cheerful, old man," he said. "Every minute now you are closer to home. You sail lighter for the loss of forty pounds."

He knew quite well the pattern of what could happen when he reached the inner part of the current. But there was nothing to be done now.

"Yes there is," he said aloud. "I can lash my knife to the butt of one of the oars."

So he did that with the tiller under his arm and the sheet of the sail under his foot.

"Now," he said. "I am still an old man. But I am not unarmed."

The breeze was fresh now and he sailed on well. He watched only the forward part of the fish and some of his hope returned. It is silly not to hope, he thought.

Besides I believe it is a sin. Do not think about sin, he thought. There are enough problems now without sin. Also I have no understanding of it.

I have no understanding of it and I am not sure that I believe in it. Perhaps it was a sin to kill the fish. I suppose it was even though I did it to keep me alive and feed many people. But then everything is a sin. Do not think about sin. It is much too late for that and there are people who are paid to do it. Let them think about it. You were born to be a fisherman as the fish was born to be a fish. San Pedro was a fisherman as was the father of the great DiMaggio.

But he liked to think about all things that he was involved in and since there was nothing to read and he did not have a radio, he thought much and he kept on thinking about sin. You did not kill the fish only to keep alive and to sell for food, he thought. You killed him for pride and because you are a fisherman. You loved him when he was alive and you loved him after. If you love him, it is not a sin to kill him. Or is it more?

"You think too much, old man," he said aloud.

But you enjoyed killing the **dentuso**, he thought. He lives on the live fish as you do. He is not a scavenger nor just a moving appetite as some sharks are. He is beautiful and noble and knows no fear of anything.

"I killed him in self-defense," the old man said aloud. "And I killed him well."

Besides, he thought, everything kills everything else in

some way. Fishing kills me exactly as it keeps me alive. The boy keeps me alive, he thought. I must not deceive myself too much.

He leaned over the side and pulled loose a piece of the meat of the fish where the shark had cut him. He chewed it and noted its quality and its good taste. It was firm and juicy, like meat, but it was not red. There was no stringiness in it and he knew that it would bring the highest price In the market. But there was no way to keep its scent out of the water and the old man knew that a very hard time was coming.

Chapter 24
The Two Sharks

The breeze was steady. It had backed a little further into the north-east and he knew that meant that it would not fall off. The old man looked ahead of him but he could see no sails nor could he see the hull nor the smoke of any ship. There were only the flying fish that went up from his bow sailing away to either side and the yellow patches of Gulf weed. He could not even see a bird.

He had sailed for two hours, resting in the stern and sometimes chewing a bit of the meat from the marlin, trying to rest and to be strong, when he saw the first of the two sharks. "Ay," he said aloud. There is no translation for this word and perhaps it is just a noise such as a man might make, involuntarily, feeling the nail go through his hands and into the wood.

"**Galanos**," he said aloud. He had seen the second fin now coming up behind the first and had identified them as shovel-nosed sharks by the brown, triangular fin and the sweeping movements of the tail. They had the scent and were excited and in the stupidity of their great hunger they were losing and finding the scent in their excitement. But they were closing all the time.

The old man made the sheet fast and jammed the tiller. Then he took up the oar with the knife lashed to it. He lifted it as lightly as he could because his hands rebelled at the pain. Then he opened and closed them on it lightly to loosen them. He closed them firmly so they would take the pain now and would not flinch and watched the sharks come. He could see their wide, flattened, shovel-pointed heads now and their white tipped wide pectoral fins. They were hateful sharks, bad smelling, scavengers as well as killers, and when they were hungry they would bite at an oar or the rudder of a boat. It was these sharks that would cut the turtles' legs and flippers off when the turtles were asleep on the surface, and they would hit a man in the water, if they were hungry, even if the man had no smell of fish blood nor of fish slime on him.

"Ay," the old man said. "**Galanos**. Come on **galanos**."

They came. But they did not come as the Mako had come. One turned and went out of sight under the skiff and the old man could feel the skiff shake as he jerked and pulled on the fish. The other watched the old man with his slitted yellow eyes and then came in fast with his half circle of jaws wide to hit the fish where he had already been bitten. The line showed clearly on the top of his brown head and back where the brain joined the spinal cord and the old man drove the knife on the oar into the juncture, withdrew it, and drove it in again into the shark's yellow cat-like eyes. The shark let go of the fish and slid down, swallowing what he had taken as he died.

The skiff was still shaking with the destruction the other shark was doing to the fish and the old man let go the sheet so that the skiff would swing broadside and bring the shark out from under. When he saw the shark he leaned over the side and punched at him. He hit only meat and the hide was set hard and he barely got the knife in. The blow hurt not only his hands but his shoulder too. But the shark came up fast with his head out and the old man hit him squarely in the center of his flat-topped head as his nose came out of water and lay against the fish. The old man withdrew the blade and punched the shark exactly in the same spot again. He still hung to the fish with his jaws hooked and the old man stabbed him in his left eye. The shark still hung there.

"No?" the old man said and he drove the blade between

the vertebrae and the brain. It was an easy shot now and he felt the cartilage sever. The old man reversed the oar and put the blade between the shark's jaws to open them. He twisted the blade and as the shark slid loose he said, "Go on, **galano**. Slide down a mile deep. Go see your friend, or maybe it's your mother."

The old man wiped the blade of his knife and laid down the oar. Then he found the sheet and the sail filled and he brought the skiff onto her course.

Chapter 25
The Broken Knife

"They must have taken a quarter of him and of the best meat," he said aloud. "I wish it were a dream and that I had never hooked him. I'm sorry about it, fish. It makes everything wrong." He stopped and he did not want to look at the fish now. Drained of blood and awash he looked the colour of the silver backing of a minor and his stripes still showed.

"I shouldn't have gone out so far, fish," he said. "Neither for you nor for me. I'm sorry, fish."

Now, he said to himself. Look to the lashing on the knife and see if it has been cut. Then get your hand in order because there still is more to come.

"I wish I had a stone for the knife," the old man said after he had checked the lashing on the oar butt. "I should have brought a stone." You should have brought many things, he thought. But you did not bring them, old man. Now is no time to think of what you do not have. Think of what you can do with what there is.

"You give me much good counsel," he said aloud. "I'm tired of it."

He held the tiller under his arm and soaked both his hands in the water as the skiff drove forward.

"God knows how much that last one took," he said.

"But she's much lighter now." He did not want to think of the mutilated under-side of the fish. He knew that each of the jerking bumps of the shark had been meat torn away and that the fish now made a trail for all sharks as wide as a highway through the sea.

He was a fish to keep a man all winter, he thought. Don't think of that. Just rest and try to get your hands in shape to defend what is left of him. The blood smell from my hands means nothing now with all that scent in the water. Besides they do not bleed much. There is nothing cut that means anything. The bleeding may keep the left from cramping. What can I think of now? he thought. Nothing. I must think of nothing and wait for the next ones. I wish it had really been a dream, he thought. But who knows? It might have turned out well.

The next shark that came was a single shovelnose. He came like a pig to the trough if a pig had a mouth so wide that you could put your head in it. The old man let him hit the fish and then drove the knife on the oar down into his brain. But the shark jerked backwards as he rolled and the knife blade snapped.

The old man settled himself to steer. He did not even watch the big shark sinking slowly in the water, showing first life-size, then small, then tiny. That always fascinated the old man. But he did not even watch it now.

"I have the gaff now," he said. "But it will do no good. I have the two oars and the tiller and the short club."

Now they have beaten me, he thought. I am too old to club sharks to death. But I will try it as long as I have the oars and the short club and the tiller. He put his hands in the water again to soak them. It was getting late in the afternoon and he saw nothing but the sea and the sky. There was more wind in the sky than there had been, and soon he hoped that he would see land.

"You're tired, old man," he said. "You're tired inside."

The sharks did not hit him again until just before sunset. The old man saw the brown fins coming along the wide trail the fish must make in the water. They were not even quartering on the scent. They were headed straight for the skiff swimming side by side.

He jammed the tiller, made the sheet fast and reached under the stem for the club. It was an oar handle from a broken oar sawed off to about two and a half feet in length. He could only use it effectively with one hand because of the grip of the handle and he took good hold of it with his right hand, flexing his hand on it, as he watched the sharks come. They were both **galanos**.

I must let the first one get a good hold and hit him on the point of the nose or straight across the top of the head, he thought. The two sharks closed together and as he saw the one nearest him open his jaws and sink them into the silver side of the fish, he raised the club high and brought it down heavy and slamming onto the top of the shark's broad head. He felt the rubbery solidity as the club came down. But he felt the rigidity of bone too and he struck the shark once more hard across the point of the nose as he slid down from the fish.

The other shark had been in and out and now came in again with his jaws wide. The old man could see pieces of the meat of the fish spilling white from the corner of his jaws as he bumped the fish and closed his jaws. He swung at him and hit only the head and the shark looked at him and wrenched the meat loose. The old man swung the club down on him again as he slipped away to swallow and hit only the heavy solid rubberiness.

"Come on, **galano**," the old man said. "Come in again."

The shark came in a rush and the old man hit him as he shut his jaws. He hit him solidly and from as high up as he could raise the club. This time he felt the bone at the base of the brain and he hit him again in the same place while the shark tore the meat loose sluggishly and slid down from the fish.

The old man watched for him to come again but neither shark showed. Then he saw one on the surface swimming in circles. He did not see the fin of the other. I could not expect to kill them, he thought. I could have in my time. But I have hurt them both badly and neither one can feel very good. If I could have used a bat with two hands I could have killed the first one surely. Even now, he thought.

Chapter 26
Half of the Fish

He did not want to look at the fish. He knew that half of him had been destroyed. The sun had gone down while he had been in the fight with the sharks.

"It will be dark soon," he said. "Then I should see the glow of Havana. If I am too far to the eastward I will see the lights of one of the new beaches."

I cannot be too far out now, he thought. I hope no one has been too worried. There is only the boy to worry, of course. But I am sure he would have confidence. Many of the older fishermen will worry. Many others too, he thought. I live in a good town.

He could not talk to the fish anymore because the fish had been ruined too badly. Then something came into his head.

"Half fish," he said. "Fish that you were. I am sorry that I went too far out. I ruined us both. But we have killed many sharks, you and I, and ruined many others. How many did you ever kill, old fish? You do not have that spear on your head for nothing."

He liked to think of the fish and what he could do to a shark if he were swimming free. I should have chopped the bill off to fight them with, he thought. But there was no hatchet and then there was no knife. But if I had, and could have lashed it to an oar butt, what a weapon. Then we might have fought them together. What will you do now if they come in the night? What can you do?

"Fight them," he said. "I'll fight them until I die."

But in the dark now and no glow showing and no lights and only the wind and the steady pull of the sail he felt that perhaps he was already dead. He put his two hands together and felt the palms. They were not dead and he could bring the pain of life by simply opening and closing them. He leaned his back against the stern and knew he was not dead. His shoulders told him.

I have all those prayers I promised if I caught the fish, he thought. But I am too tired to say them now. I better get the sack and put it over my shoulders.

He lay in the stern and steered and watched for the glow to come in the sky. I have half of him, he thought. Maybe I'll have the luck to bring the forward half in. I should have some luck. No, he said. You violated your luck when you went too far outside.

"Don't be silly," he said aloud. "And keep awake and steer. You may have much luck yet."

"I'd like to buy some if there's any place they sell it," he said.

What could I buy it with? he asked himself. Could I buy it with a lost harpoon and a broken knife and two bad hands?

"You might," he said. "You tried to buy it with eighty-four days at sea. They nearly sold it to you too."

I must not think nonsense, he thought. Luck is a thing that comes in many forms and who can recognize her? I would take some though in any form and pay what they asked. I wish I could see the glow from the lights, he thought. I wish too many things. But that is the thing I wish for now. He tried to settle more comfortably to steer and from his pain he knew he was not dead.

Chapter 27
The Last Fight

He saw the reflected glare of the lights of the city at what must have been around ten o'clock at night. They were only perceptible at first as the light is in the sky before the moon rises. Then they were steady to see across the ocean which was rough now with the increasing breeze. He steered inside of the glow and he thought that now, soon, he must hit the edge of the stream.

Now it is over, he thought. They will probably hit me again. But what can a man do against them in the dark without a weapon? He was stiff and sore now and his wounds and all of the strained parts of his body hurt with the cold of the night. I hope I do not have to fight again, he thought. I hope so much I do not have to fight again.

But by midnight he fought and this time he knew the fight was useless. They came in a pack and he could only see the lines in the water that their fins made and their phosphorescence as they threw themselves on the fish. He clubbed at heads and heard the jaws chop and the shaking of the skiff as they took hold below. He clubbed desperately at what he could only feel and hear and he felt something seize the club and it was gone.

He jerked the tiller free from the rudder and beat and chopped with it, holding it in both hands and driving it down again and again. But they were up to the bow now and driving in one after the other and together, tearing off the pieces of meat that showed glowing below the sea as they turned to come once more.

One came, finally, against the head itself and he knew that it was over. He swung the tiller across the shark's head where the jaws were caught in the heaviness of the fish's head which would not tear. He swung it once and twice and again. He heard the tiller break and he lunged at the shark with the splintered butt. He felt it go in and knowing it was sharp he drove it in again. The shark let go and rolled away. That was the last shark of the pack that came. There was nothing more for them to eat.

The old man could hardly breathe now and he felt a strange taste in his mouth. It was coppery and sweet and he was afraid of it for a moment. But there was not much of it. He spat into the ocean and said, "Eat that, **galanos**. And make a dream you've killed a man."

He knew he was beaten now finally and without remedy and he went back to the stern and found the jagged end of the tiller would fit in the slot of the rudder well enough for him to steer. He settled the sack around his shoulders and put the skiff on her course.

He sailed lightly now and he had no thoughts nor any feelings of any kind. He was past everything now and he sailed the skiff to make his home port as well and as intelligently as he could. In the night sharks hit the carcass as someone might pick up crumbs from the table. The old man paid no attention to them and did not pay any attention to anything except steering. He only noticed how lightly and how well the skiff sailed now there was no great weight beside her.

She's good, he thought. She is sound and not harmed in any way except for the tiller. That is easily replaced. He could feel he was inside the current now and he could see the lights of the beach colonies along the shore. He knew where he was now and it was nothing to get home.

The wind is our friend, anyway, he thought. Then he added, sometimes. And the great sea with our friends and our enemies. And bed, he thought. Bed is my friend. Just bed, he thought. Bed will be a great thing. It is easy when you are beaten, he thought. I never knew how easy it was. And what beat you, he thought.

"Nothing," he said aloud. "I went out too far."

When he sailed into the little harbour the lights of the Terrace were out and he knew everyone was in bed. The breeze had risen steadily and was blowing strongly now. It was quiet in the harbour though and he sailed up onto the little patch of shingle below the rocks. There was no one to help him so he pulled the boat up as far as he could. Then he stepped out and made her fast to a rock.

He unstepped the mast and furled the sail and tied it. Then he shouldered the mast and started to climb. It was then he knew the depth of his tiredness. He stopped for a moment and looked back and saw in the reflection from the street light the great tail of the fish standing up well behind the skiff's stern. He saw the white naked line of his backbone and the dark mass of the head with the projecting bill and all the nakedness between.

He started to climb again and at the top he fell and lay for some time with the mast across his shoulder. He tried to get up. But it was too difficult and he sat there with the mast on his shoulder and looked at the road. A cat passed on the far side going about its business and the old man watched it. Then he just watched the road.

Finally he put the mast down and stood up. He picked the mast up and put it on his shoulder and started up the road. He had to sit down five times before he reached his shack. Inside the shack he leaned the mast against the wall. In the dark he found a water bottle and took a drink. Then he lay down on the bed. He pulled the blanket over his shoulders and then over his back and legs and he slept face down on the newspapers with his arms out straight and the palms of his hands up.

Chapter 28
At Home

He was asleep when the boy looked in the door in the morning. It was blowing so hard that the drifting-boats would not be going out and the boy had slept late and then come to the old man's shack as he had come each morning. The boy saw that the old man was breathing and then he saw the old man's hands and he started to cry. He went out very quietly to go to bring some coffee and all the way down the road he was crying.

Many fishermen were around the skiff looking at what was lashed beside it and one was in the water, his trousers rolled up, measuring the skeleton with a length of line. The boy did not go down. He had been there before and one of the fishermen was looking after the skiff for him.

"How is he?" one of the fishermen shouted. "Sleeping," the boy called. He did not care that they saw him crying.

"Let no one disturb him."

"He was eighteen feet from nose to tail," the fisherman who was measuring him called.

"I believe it," the boy said.

He went into the Terrace and asked for a can of coffee.

"Hot and with plenty of milk and sugar in it."

"Anything more?"

"No. Afterwards I will see what he can eat."

"What a fish it was," the proprietor said. "There has never been such a fish. Those were two fine fish you took yesterday too."

"Damn my fish," the boy said and he started to cry again.

"Do you want a drink of any kind?" the proprietor asked.

"No," the boy said. "Tell them not to bother Santiago. I'll be back."

"Tell him how sorry I am."

"Thanks," the boy said.

The boy carried the hot can of coffee up to the old man's shack and sat by him until

he woke. Once it looked as though he were waking. But he had gone back into heavy sleep and the boy had gone across the road to borrow some wood to heat the coffee. Finally the old man woke.

"Don't sit up," the boy said. "Drink this."

He poured some of the coffee in a glass. The old man took it and drank it.

"They beat me, Manolin," he said. "They truly beat me."

"He didn't beat you. Not the fish."

"No. Truly. It was afterwards."

"Pedrico is looking after the skiff and the gear. What do you want done with the head?"

"Let Pedrico chop it up to use in fish traps."

"And the spear?"

"You keep it if you want it."

"I want it," the boy said. "Now we must make our plans

about the other things."

"Did they search for me?"

"Of course. With coast guard and with planes."

"The ocean is very big and a skiff is small and hard to see," the old man said. He noticed how pleasant it was to have someone to talk to instead of speaking only to himself and to the sea.

"I missed you," he said. "What did you catch?"

"One the first day. One the second and two the third."

"Very good."

"Now we fish together again."

"No. I am not lucky. I am not lucky anymore."

"The hell with luck," the boy said. "I'll bring the luck with me."

"What will your family say?"

"I do not care. I caught two yesterday. But we will fish together now for I still have much to learn."

"We must get a good killing lance and always have it on board. You can make the blade from a spring leaf from an old Ford. We can grind it in Guanabacoa. It should be sharp and not tempered so it will break. My knife broke."

"I'll get another knife and have the spring ground."

How many days of heavy **brisa** have we?"

"Maybe three. Maybe more."

"I will have everything in order," the boy said. "You get your hands well old man."

"I know how to care for them. In the night I spat something strange and felt something in my chest was broken."

"Get that well too," the boy said. "Lie down, old man, and I will bring you your clean shirt. And something to eat."

"Bring any of the papers of the time that I was gone," the old man said.

"You must get well fast for there is much that I can learn and you can teach me everything. How much did you suffer?"

"Plenty," the old man said.

"I'll bring the food and the papers," the boy said. "Rest well, old man. I will bring stuff from the drugstore for your hands."

"Don't forget to tell Pedrico the head is his."

"No. I will remember."

As the boy went out the door and down the worn coral rock road he was crying again. That afternoon there was a party of tourists at the Terrace and looking down in the water among the empty beer cans and dead barracudas a woman saw a great long white spine with a huge tail at the end that lifted and swung with the tide while the east wind blew a heavy steady sea outside the entrance to the harbour.

"What's that?" she asked a waiter and pointed to the long backbone of the great fish that was now just garbage waiting to go out with the tide.

"Tiburon," the waiter said. "Shark." He was meaning to

explain what had happened.

"I didn't know sharks had such handsome, beautifully formed tails."

"I didn't either," her male companion said.

Up the road, in his shack, the old man was sleeping again. He was still sleeping on his face and the boy was sitting by him watching him. The old man was dreaming about the lions.

여기까지 오신 여러분께 아낌없는 찬사를 보냅니다. "레벨 5까지 올라오시느라, 고생 많으셨습니다!" 자, 이제 내려갈 일만 남았습니다. 끝난 게 아니냐고요? 지금까지의 과정을 '등산'이라고 생각해 보세요. 이제 하산을 하셔야 합니다.

『단계 영어』에서 하산이란, 복잡하고 어려운 문장이 어떻게 간결하고 쉬운 문장으로 변하는지를 체감하는 것입니다. 단계를 내려가며 읽으면, 요약적 사고를 키우는 데 도움이 됩니다. 레벨5부터 시작하실 필요는 없습니다. 레벨 4부터 천천히 내려가세요. 그렇다고 챕터까지 거꾸로 읽진 마시고, 레벨만 한 단계씩 내려가며 읽어 보세요.

이렇게 읽으시면, 여러분은 '노인과 바다' 원서를 총 아홉 번 읽은 것이 됩니다. 이 정도면 노인과 바다 원서를 정복하는 용감한 독자가 되지 않겠어요?

이 책을 통한 학습을 원한다면, '동일 챕터별 읽기'를 강력히 추천합니다. 같은 챕터를 다른 레벨로 읽으며, 어휘와 문장 구조를 집중적으로 학습해보세요. 이렇게 하면, 짧은 시간 안에 같은 내용을 다양한 난이도로 접하며, 영어 실력을 한층 업그레이드할 수 있습니다.

'노인과 바다' 다음에는 '마지막 잎새'와 '동물 농장'이 나올 예정입니다. 좀 더 쉬운 영어 읽기를 원하시는 분들은 『단계 영어 잠자는 공주』와 『단계 영어 백설 공주』를 추천합니다. 앞으로 나올 단계 영어를 통해, 일반 영어 원서도 부담 없이 읽을 그 날을 기대해봅시다.

"단계 영어"는 세계문학과 명작을 중심으로 제작될 예정입니다.
신간에 대한 최신 정보는 카카오 채널 @동행출판사에서 받으실 수 있습니다.
다음 "단계 영어"에서 만나 뵙겠습니다.